A Deadly Game of TUG OF WAR

The Kelsey Smith-Briggs Story

T0117305

Craig Key

New York

A Deadly Game of Tug of War

By Craig Key

ISBN: 978-1-60037-311-4 (Paperback)
ISBN: 978-1-60037-312-1 (Hardcover)

Published by:

MORGAN · JAMES
THE ENTREPRENEURIAL PUBLISHER
www.morganjamespublishing.com

Morgan James Publishing, LLC
1225 Franklin Ave. Suite 325
Garden City, NY 11530-1693
800.485.4943
www.MorganJamesPublishing.com

Cover & Interior Design by:

Megan Johnson
Johnson2Design
www.Johnson2Design.com
megan@Johnson2Design.com

Editing by:

Jody Ortiz

This book is dedicated to my wife, Dana,
our beautiful daughters, and our extended family.
Your love and support has kept me going through
the months of media scrutiny.
Thank you and I love you,
Craig

Kelsey Smith-Briggs was a beautiful blond-haired, blue-eyed, 2-year-old little girl whose death sent shock waves of anguish and anger throughout the State of Oklahoma. As the news of her violent death following child abuse documented by the Department of Human Services and the court system began to unfold, citizens demanded to know who was responsible for failing to protect Kelsey. They wanted not only the perpetrator of her murder punished, but also those involved in the juvenile justice system to be held accountable for allowing the child to be returned to persons who were suspected of causing the abuse. Ultimately, the blame for "the system" failing Kelsey became focused on the Judge who signed the order returning Kelsey to the home of her mother. Four months later, she was rushed to the hospital where she died as the result of blunt force trauma to her abdomen.

The subsequent public outcry resulted in the vilification of the author of this book, Associate District Judge Craig Key, a man who had sought public office in order to devote himself to the protection of our most vulnerable citizens, the children. Instead, his dream ended in a nightmare of self-reproach, enduring the public's scorn and blame for the death of a child, and ultimately his defeat for re-election.

Having spent more than forty years as a police officer, assistant district attorney, criminal defense lawyer, and legal analyst, I have seen my share of children like Kelsey who are destined for tragedy, seemingly from birth. As you read this book, it will become apparent the true responsibility for her death lies with those who had the highest duty to protect her; her mother, father, and family. Like far too many children, she became not a precious blessing to be cherished, but a helpless victim in a brutal child custody battle between two families. Although all involved professed to love her, instead they used Kelsey as a club to wield against the opposing family. She became the ultimate prize in a fight which was never to end, not even with her death.

When signs of abuse to Kelsey began to be noted and reported to the child protection division of the Department of Human Services and the court system the mother's family blamed the father, and his family pointed at the mother. In the midst of this swearing match and escalating signs of abuse, Kelsey was removed from both parents and a safe haven within the extended family was sought. Child care professionals, social services, and voluntary child advocates kept a daily watch upon her welfare, but still there were frequent "accidental" injuries documented regarding Kelsey, and innocent explanations of childhood mishaps were supplied and reported to the court. Kelsey was too young to tell anyone about what was really happening or who was hurting her.

Her father was eventually deployed to fight in Iraq and her mother was given a legally required "treatment plan" designed to correct deficiencies and to effectuate a safe reunion between Kelsey and her mother. The mother completed the plan and the child was assimilated back into her home, which now included a step-father. Monitoring continued until the fateful day on which Kelsey was hurt for the last time.

No one in Kelsey's family loved her enough to put aside their mutual hatred, and now the prize they fought tooth and claw for, is forever lost; shame on them all.

By: Irven Box, Attorney and Media Legal Analyst

TABLE OF CONTENTS

The untimely death of a child is the most difficult and anguishing event any family should have to endure. My thoughts, prayers, and sympathy are with every member of Kelsey's families. Even as the Briggs family made negative comments about myself, they have remained in my thoughts and prayers, and my deepest sympathies are extended to them. While I have had a chance to speak in public with certain members of the Smith family, I keep each member of that family in my thoughts as well. At times, my mind races to Michael Porter's two children, and finally, to Michael Porter and Raye Dawn Smith's baby born shortly after Kelsey's tragedy. I attempt to show my respect and dignity for all family members, while providing an accurate account of the events that transpired during Kelsey's short life and ultimate death.

The tug-of-war for Kelsey Smith-Briggs began with two birth announcements and ended with two obituaries and two funerals. In her short two and a half years, Kelsey struggled to find peace as the maternal and paternal sides of her family wrestled each other for her custody and could not share her love. Even after Kelsey's death, she is unable to rest, due to the constant fighting between her families.

The story of her short life and ultimate death, along with the search for her real killer is not an easy story to tell. The subject matter, alone, is heartbreaking; the memories are overwhelming; the guilt is enough to tear out your gut. However, it is one that must be told in order to bring light to the facts in the case to dispel any of the rumors and innuendos that have run rampant throughout the State of Oklahoma, and on a larger scale, nationally.

There is no doubt that Kelsey Smith-Briggs was loved by all members of each family. However, the tug-of-war over Kelsey ultimately cost her life. If her families had worked together to raise Kelsey, instead of fighting each other, costly mistakes may have been avoided.

I am telling this story from my perspective as the trial judge on this case. Some of the facts mentioned have come to light since Kelsey's death; I did not know the entire history that surrounded this case when I saw Kelsey's families in my courtroom; I did not know what was happening behind the scenes at the time of the trials, but I am providing everything to you, the reader, to let you be the judge.

Although some of the language used in this book may be seen as legalistic, uncaring, or as if I am judgmental toward certain key players in this case, that is not the intention of this book. I am portraying this case from the viewpoint of my job as a judge.

In the final pages of this book you can learn more about my ideas for reform in our area that will help those like Kelsey find hope in their lives filled with abuse and turmoil. This is the story of Kelsey Shelton Smith-Briggs...

CHAPTER ONE

October 11, 2005
The Day Kelsey Died

It was a nice, cool, windy fall day in the small, quiet town of Chandler, Oklahoma. This sleepy little town is tucked away along historic Route 66 square in the American heartland. In fact, Route 66 is the main street in town and goes right in front of the courthouse square. It's where I grew up, where my family settled during the Land Run of 1891, and until recently, where I served as the Associate District Judge of Lincoln County.

But all that was about to change…

The day started out as any other. After we all got ready for our day, I kissed my wife, Dana, goodbye and dropped our four daughters off at school on my way to the courthouse. I spent the morning hearing small claims cases and protective orders, and in the afternoon my friend, Tipper, and I headed out to my cousin's farm to work a load of cattle I had just purchased.

I decided to get into the cattle business as an outlet, a pressure release from the daily horror stories you hear as judge. I could sort through my day and refocus on what mattered most to me and my family. I would try to make sense of the images and stories of the abused and neglected children, the adults who were drug abusers, the divorce cases, and everything that I saw on a daily basis in my courtroom. Driving through the pasture, tending cattle had become my oasis, my escape.

We were getting ready to head the cattle into the lane and up to the chute when one cow, a big black Brangus, jumped out of the lane and ran back into the pen. It took some time, but we finally managed to get her back in line. Ironically, she was tagged as the number 13 cow. As a result of jumping over the lane, she wrenched her hip and would lie in the woods on the back corner of my farm for the next few months. I took protein cubes to her, trying to nurse her back to health.

Number 13 and I have been through a lot together. She's the one cow that always seemed to separate from the herd, and she's the one I discussed the day with as I mulled over the decisions I made in and out of the courtroom.

On that brisk fall day, as I relished in the peace and tranquility that farming provides, I had no idea what was going on just 14 miles away in Meeker, another small town south of Chandler on Highway 18.

We had just finished vaccinating and tagging the cows and had released them on my farm. It was 5:33pm, and I was driving through Chandler and getting ready to go over and pay my cousin for the cows. I was on Route 66 where it turns to head straight west when my cell phone rang and David, a supervisor for the local Department of Human Services (DHS) office informed me that Kelsey Smith-Briggs had died in the Prague hospital that day.

The image of the two-year-old little girl popped into my head and I wondered if I had heard him correctly. I remembered her playing in the courthouse lobby during her court case.

I took a break on the first day of the court hearing in June. The courthouse had already closed. It was around 5:15pm when I walked through the courthouse to get a Coke. Instead of going to the machine just outside my office door, I went all the way to the other side of the courthouse to the lobby where Kelsey was playing. Throughout the bitter custody battle I had heard two completely different stories of her behavior, and I wanted to see her for myself. She was running around playing. She looked like a totally normal child, no bruises, nothing. She had been hopping around, almost bubbly.

As the road blurred ahead of me, her sweet cherub smile, blonde hair, and blue eyes were all I could see in front of me. *She's not dead! She's a child, a baby! It's not possible!* I fought to keep control of the wheel. It just didn't make sense! I couldn't believe what David was telling me. It wasn't possible!

I pulled into the parking lot of the old ice company and put the truck in park, turning off the ignition. My mind raced as I tried to make sense of what he had said. I felt a heavy pressure on my chest and my head was spinning. My stomach was nauseous and every breath labored and shallow.

It felt as if someone had called and told me that one of my own children had died. My job as judge was to protect those children whose cases were presented in my courtroom. I had done all I could to protect Kelsey, just as I would have done if she had been my own child.

Emotions flooded over me and I felt lost, alone, and confused. The biggest question in my mind was the cause of death. Initially, those who had been watching the case all thought it was from the seizures she had been experiencing recently. That moment was the lowest feeling I had ever felt in my life.

The role of protector and mentor was one I took personally for every single child that came into my courtroom. I felt since they were wards of my court, which is what the law provides, they were just as precious to me as if they were my own. I knew each child by name, and could recall every detail of their file without looking.

I took my job seriously, and the decisions that I made about each case reflected the care and concern I felt for each child, regardless of their background. The emotional weight of losing a child I had sworn to protect was almost too much to bear. I became literally sick and my mind raced with sorrow, doubt, and concern.

None of the evidence, allegations, or testimony that I had seen from the time I had made the decision to return Kelsey to the custody of her mother, Raye Dawn Smith in June, until October 11th had caused me to doubt whether or not I made the right decision. I had questioned DHS workers on several occasions to find out how Kelsey was doing, and I was continuously told she was doing well and that she was continuing to grow her hair back and gain weight.

I informed all of the involved agencies that if there was anything they were concerned about, they needed to let me know. If I had even the slightest idea that she wasn't doing well, I would have pulled her out of her mother's home immediately. However, that thought never came up as a result of any of the conversations I had with DHS or anyone else involved in the case.

In fact, the placement of Kelsey in Raye Dawn's home was going so well that at the September 8th hearing to stop the visitation of the paternal side of the family, the Assistant District Attorney and Kelsey's court appointed attorney wanted to dismiss the entire case against Raye Dawn. Such a dismissal agreed upon by all parties would have meant that the District Attorney (DA), Department of Human Services (DHS), Comprehensive Home Based Services (CHBS), Court Appointed Special Advocates (CASA), everyone, would have ceased having any contact with the child and her family. That's how well her reunion with her mother was going.

> The September 8th hearing was one that should have been a fight for the Briggs family to retain their visitation. However, nobody from that family showed up. Further details are given in Chapter Fifteen.

I had worked within the confines of the legal system, and had based my decision on the testimony and evidence presented to me in court and what I was being told by those charged with watching the case. That's all I had to go on, and everything I'd seen confirmed that although this case did involve allegations of child abuse, there was no definite perpetrator identified. It was apparent to anyone who was involved in investigating the case that Raye Dawn loved and wanted Kelsey. She fully cooperated with the authorities to gain back custody of her child. Further evidence was the fact that even after the June hearing, Raye Dawn continued her complete cooperation with the agencies that watched out for Kelsey.

What I had seen from the bench told me that the case was clearly an emotionally charged child custody case, with conflicting allegations of abuse throughout. I thought that giving Kelsey back to Raye Dawn would end the nightmare the child was experiencing, but when David told me she was dead, I didn't see that coming at all. It was as if I had entered the *Twilight Zone*. DHS (Department of Human Services, Oklahoma's division of child protective services) supervisors and case workers found the turn of events just as disturbing.

After a few minutes of silence, tears, and outcries for an explanation of what could have possibly happened, I turned my attention back to David. He's a smooth dressing guy, an ordained minister, and truly a man of God.

David and I took a moment and said a prayer for Kelsey and her family. Neither of us had lost a child, and we couldn't even imagine the sorrow and pain those who loved her must have been facing. We prayed for peace for little Kelsey and for healing for her family.

I asked David how he was doing. I imagined he was experiencing the same feelings I was at that point. He told me he was beyond broken over the situation. He was astonished and stunned that all of our efforts to ensure Kelsey was in a loving secure environment could have been ripped to shreds. Like me, he wondered what could have happened to cause her death.

Next I asked about Yolanda, Kelsey's case worker. She had day-to-day contact with Kelsey and had gotten close to the little girl during all that had transpired. The best thing about Yolanda is that she has a heart of gold. I could always count on her compassion to make decisions in the best interest of the child. I knew that she too would be grieving and questioning how something like this could have happened. There was hardly a day that went by that she didn't talk to Kelsey and her mother, Raye Dawn, on the phone from the time Kelsey had returned home to her mother in June until her death in October, 2005.

To this day, Yolanda still has phone messages on her answering machine at work that Kelsey had left for her. Kelsey put Easter stickers on the window of her office, and those stickers remain, almost two years later.

> To this day, Yolanda still has phone messages on her answering machine at work that Kelsey had left for her.

Kelsey's death did not make sense to David or Yolanda. DHS had been so involved and they were closely monitoring this case. How could something like this happen right under their noses and to a child who was being visited, talked to, or observed practically every day? DHS workers or other agencies were in Kelsey's home regularly. The day she died one of the agency workers had visited the home just two hours before her death.

They searched for signs of abuse and nobody ever saw anything that raised concerns about Kelsey's welfare or gave them cause to remove her from her mother's home.

> They searched for signs of abuse and nobody ever saw anything that raised concerns about Kelsey's welfare or gave them cause to remove her from her mother's home.

David informed me that Yolanda was taking the tragedy very hard. She has always worked so diligently for all the children on her caseload, and is the sweetest lady going. She's a lovely blonde lady, and is usually smiling and happy, but Kelsey's death really hit her hard and she suffered from uncontrollable sobbing for at least the first four or five days. That first day she was an emotional mess! Although I felt as if Kelsey was my own because she was my ward, Yolanda had spent countless hours with her, loved her, and had bonded with her. The bond was mutual. During one of Yolanda's breakdowns she confided in me that Kelsey called her every night on her cell phone to tell her goodnight. The toddler refused to go to bed before she spoke with Yolanda. After Kelsey's death she questioned what happened and felt, as we all did, responsible because she hadn't prevented her death.

Initially, DHS believed her death was a result a seizure disorder Kelsey had been experiencing. In early September the Assistant District Attorney handling Kelsey's case filed a motion with a doctor's statement attached, asking me to stop all paternal family visitation. At the direction of a doctor, it was decided by those watching the case that Kelsey's environment needed to be completely controlled. They wanted to monitor who she was around in order to determine what was triggering her seizures. DHS and the doctor recognized that the child had been in an epic struggle, a tug of war, an absolutely brutal custody battle, and they had to narrow her seizures down to a particular place and time so they could determine the cause.

I was really troubled by the fact that the paternal family was provided notice of the hearing, and yet no one bothered to show up on the day of the proceedings. Even their attorney was absent. *Why not show up?* It didn't make sense to me that they would fight so hard to keep Kelsey away from Raye Dawn and then not even bother to show up when there was a possibility that their visitation rights could be taken away. This reaffirmed my belief that I had made the right decision in returning Kelsey to Raye Dawn, and that everything was on the right track.

> I was really troubled by the fact that the paternal family was provided notice of the hearing, and yet no one bothered to show up on the day of the proceedings.

After hanging up with David I cleared my head enough to drive home. I walked into my house a broken man, devastated by grief. That evening I was on the phone a great deal with various DHS workers who were trying to find out what to do in regards to the other children in Raye Dawn's home.

On April 18, 2005, Raye Dawn married Michael Porter. He had custody of his nine-year-old daughter and more than regular visitation with his two-year-old son. At this point, he was not a suspect to any abuse charges or in Kelsey's death. As is common in these types of cases, the authorities took precautions to safeguard his two children who had been residing in the home. Arrangements were made for his son to go back home to his mother, and his daughter went with another relative until there was time to process what had happened, find out the cause of death, and decide what to do in the case.

The thing that I remember the most about that night was lying in bed and never sleeping, but simply just praying that the decisions everyone had made did not cost Kelsey's life. We had looked at everything we had collected in the way of evidence and testimonies in order to make the best decision we could make for the sake of the child. But it's impossible to make perfect decisions with imperfect information.

> It's impossible to make perfect decisions with imperfect information.

Afterthought

As you go through the pages of this book, you'll see what I mean by the imperfect information that was presented to me during the court proceedings. When two families have this kind of hatred for each other, it is not their goal to do what is best for the child, but rather to punish the other side of the family.

I replayed in my mind everything the police had told me, what the lawyers told me, what I heard in court, and what DHS had given me, and I drew a blank. It was as if I was searching for a nonexistent needle in a haystack. There just wasn't anything more I could have done with what I was given. I knew that at the time, and I know that now. But that doesn't make it any easier to swallow the truth of the matter: an innocent little girl had died and I felt responsible. *What more could have been done?* After you read this book, ask yourself the question.

As a judge, the decisions I made affected the lives of those who appeared in my courtroom, for better or worse. A decision that was right, just, and fair, and meant to protect a child from harm met with the untimely death of an innocent young girl.

The turn of events in this case has taken its toll on several families. The Smith family lost a precious child that used to light up their world. The Briggs family grieves over their bubbly granddaughter who left them way too soon. DHS and other involved agencies have been questioned about their role in this case, and workers, like Yolanda, grieve over the loss of a child who was so easy to love. My world has been turned upside down. The very thing I dedicated my life to preventing happened, and what I worked so hard to achieve in our county is unraveling before my eyes. My reputation has been tarnished and my judicial career is over. Untruths have been told, rumors have been spread, and though I've been blamed for the death of Kelsey Smith-Briggs, the true killer may be sitting in a prison cell, while the child's mom faces a court battle of her own.

It does not matter what I have suffered personally or professionally in light of the circumstances around this case. I would have given it all up to save Kelsey. A career can be rebuilt. A reputation can be mended when the truth presents itself. But a life can never be relived. It's time for the truth to be told.

Many have questioned repeatedly for a justification of my decision to return Kelsey to Raye Dawn, but I have remained tight-lipped about what happened in this infamous case. That is, until now…

A Deadly Game of Tug of War

CHAPTER TWO

January 13, 2002
Judge Craig Key - Sworn In

The desire to seek public office is something that very few people could ever understand. But anyone who has been in my shoes knows the heartache, public humiliation, and daily scrutiny that public officials must endure in order to be where they are in society. Whether you are in a small county in Oklahoma or in the heart of New York City, public officials are constantly scrutinized. The difference is that here the scrutinizing comes from your neighbors; the people who know and see you every day.

It's hard to go to the grocery store or to eat out with your family without seeing someone you dealt with in court. Either people loved me or hated me. With every decision I made, I only made half of the people I saw in my courtroom happy. That's just the result of making the decisions you have to make in following the law and ruling on the evidence before you.

Before I decided to become a judge I was a practicing attorney in Chandler, Oklahoma; an active member of the Lincoln County Public Facilities Trust Authority and the Chandler Lion's Club; served as Law Day Chairman for the Lincoln County Bar Association; served as past President of the Chandler Chamber of Commerce; and was an elder at my church. I worked hard to be a positive influence in the community I had grown up in and where I chose to raise my children.

I had earned a Bachelor of Arts degree from the University of Oklahoma (OU) with a double major in Law Enforcement Administration and History in 1989. I then went on to receive my Juris Doctor Degree from OU in 1992, and began practicing law that year.

I had a fairly quiet life that I still share today with my beautiful, loving, and supportive wife, Dana. She graduated from the University of Central Oklahoma (UCO) with a degree in Elementary Education in 1991, and taught fifth grade for several years in Texas. When we married in 2000 and began blending our families, she chose to be a stay-at-home mom to our four brilliant and wonderful daughters: Abbi (14), Macy (13), Sarah (12), and Kamryn (8).

We had been married for two years when I campaigned for judge, as our family struggled to find common ground as a unit. It was stressful blending the families. We had both been single parents of two daughters. When we married, we also became step-parents, giving us four daughters total. On the outside it must have appeared that we had it all. In reality, our lives have been far from perfect. Things have been tough in our blended family, as it can be in many families, yet we wouldn't have it any other way.

All four of the girls live with us and their non-custodial parents have visitation, so we were dealing with ex-spouses and their families when our lives went public.

At the time I ran for judge, I had first-hand experience of what it's like to share children with someone with whom you couldn't make a marriage work. It's not that our ex-families were a problem, but we knew what it felt like as parents to let go, to lose control, or have no control when the children weren't with us. It's a scary feeling not knowing what's going on when you're not around, especially if parenting styles and philosophies differ from your own.

This experience helped me to be empathetic to what those with child custody issues were experiencing. In some ways, our family experienced the drama ourselves. We've had our children cry over not being with their other parent and cry when they didn't want to leave us.

These family issues were very close to my heart, which strengthened my desire to ensure I was as careful as possible in making child custody decisions. I took that passion with me in running for judge.

Our faith has given us strength and kept us going throughout the entire election process and still keeps us going today. We were then and still are active members of the First Christian Church in Chandler, where my family has been members for over 100 years. I still serve as an elder and Dana serves as a youth leader.

I was sworn in as Associate District Judge of Lincoln County on January 13, 2003, to an overflowing courtroom. I remember praying in my chambers with my close friend, Skip Hill, along with my family just moments before going into the courtroom to take my oath. My judicial career had finally begun and I was excited about taking office and making a difference in the lives of the citizens of Lincoln County, Oklahoma. It had been a tough race against Judge David Welch, the incumbent judge I replaced. He had been in office for 16 years. Judge Welch is a good man, we just have different philosophies on the role a judge should have within his community.

My platform focused on Lincoln County's need for programs designed to help drug addicts get clean and sober, and to provide alternative punishment for misdemeanor offenders. I also wanted to develop much needed programs like Project Safe and CASA in our area for victims of domestic abuse and children.

In my newly elected position as Associate District Judge, I would oversee all types of cases. My campaign had focused on directing the implementation of mandatory community service for certain offenders and services for victims of domestic violence and child abuse. Our jurisdiction neighbored counties that had great results with similar programs. I wanted to bring such results to our county as well.

The funny thing about my election in 2002, and then my re-election campaign in 2006, was the fact that I was fully supported by most, if not all the foster parents in Lincoln County. In fact, because of my passion and drive to make a difference in the lives of Oklahoma children, many top DHS officials attended my swearing in ceremony. They were excited about the direction and focus on children's programs that I wanted to bring to our county.

In 2003, shortly after the election, Youth and Family Resources Inc., a Shawnee, Oklahoma based non-profit corporation that runs the shelter for abused children, oversees the juvenile detention center, and provides support services for both youth and family programs in Pottawatomie and Lincoln Counties, appointed me to their board. The focus of our court was to make a better life for children and stopping domestic violence. My goal was to lock up the people who posed a danger to society, and rehabilitate those with substance abuse issues so that we could help them become productive citizens again.

Prior to my election as judge in 2002, our county had absolutely no services such as community service, accountability for offenders, counseling for domestic violence victims, drug abuse counseling, and other services for families. It was through hard work from my court staff members and me that the protective and accountability programs were instituted. Before our hard work, there were no alternatives to incarceration like drug court or relationships with long-term drug and alcohol rehabilitation centers. We also brought the successful Project Safe to our county so that victims of domestic violence would have support in the courtroom and could receive counseling to help them change their positions in life.

You see, I didn't run for office to merely take up space in the courthouse; it wasn't a power issue for me, and the title had nothing to do with my drive to be a judge. I decided to become a judge because I wanted to make positive changes in people's lives. Public service, to me, is a commitment to the people you represent.

The reason I'm mentioning all of this is because the one thing that was not mentioned in any of the newspaper articles or through media coverage during the firestorm that proceeded Kelsey's death is that DHS and Lincoln County had already made great strides in working to protect our children. Throughout the state there is an enormous effort each day to ensure our children have a future. There are so many children that are saved because of the hard work and dedication of law enforcement, DHS officials, the court, and foster parents. Although it's hard to deal with the loss of even a single child, and if every single death could be prevented, the officials would find a way to make this happen. They're dedicated to the purpose of saving lives, and the amount of lives that are saved is amazing. There is no media coverage; there are no banners, no billboards - nothing is going on for the ones that are saved or for those who work long hours at minimal pay to ensure it happens.

We forget about those children who are protected each year by the hard work and dedication of individuals within the system. As judge, I wanted to increase the odds and do what was within my power to do to ensure the safety of all children in my care. Not only did I work directly with the officials to try to make a difference, I also operated differently with the children in my care. Here is a little bit about how I would run my courtroom:

As a juvenile judge in Lincoln County, my caseload would typically have four to ten special needs children under the juvenile mental health law. Those types of cases I reviewed every 28 days. There are so many of these children that came back to me like a revolving door. Every time they came back to court, I would try to have a pizza party or provide something they would want to eat. If their birthday fell within those 28 days, I would have the review on their birthday and have gifts there for them. When they came to my courtroom, there would be six to eight court personnel, who would sit down and have a soft drink or eat with them. I would come down off the bench and instead of appearing as an official with only the law in mind, I would let the children know that they meant something to me, as individuals, and it was my desire to have them succeed in life. It was my intention in doing things like that directly with the children that in their eyes we would be humanized, not just authority figures, and it would hopefully motivate them toward a positive future.

Probably the hardest part of losing my bid for re-election in 2006 has been missing the children, and seeing the positive changes made in their lives.

There was a young, 13-year-old girl who was traumatically abused as a young child by her step-brother and step-father. I reviewed her case right before my term as judge expired. After I lost, she said that she was going to run away and that I was the only one who had ever shown any care or concern for her or had worked with her. Having to sit those types of kids down and say, "Look, it's okay. I'm always here for you, because I care about you. It's how you handle these adversities that matter, and you've got to come through this," was tough for me. I wanted to make a difference and to make progress. I watched it all slip away due to the mischaracterizations and lies surrounding this case during the re-election campaign. That was really difficult to accept.

Afterthought

When voting for a public official, the general public does not take into account that there are people who are deeply affected by their choice in candidate. Judges hear cases of all types, not merely divorces, civil, and criminal cases. Once a judge swears his or her oath to uphold the law, this position could seriously alter the course for the abandoned, abused, and troubled youth in our country.

Leaving the bench has left me feeling that I have abandoned the children who needed me most, like the young girl. It has not been an easy cross to bear, wondering about the fate of those I left in the care of my successor. I have always asked people, "What would you do to make a difference?"

CHAPTER THREE

Lance and Raye Dawn Tie a Loose Knot

Raye Dawn Smith and Lance Briggs met at Meeker High School, in Meeker, Oklahoma, where Raye Dawn was on the pom squad with Lance's sister. They seemed like a happy young couple until word spread that Lance had allegedly beaten up a former girlfriend. Raye Dawn's family became worried that she had chosen the wrong sort of boy.

Raye Dawn's parents, Ray and Gayla Smith, had been married for 33 years on April 15, 2004, the day Ray Smith lost his battle against colon cancer that had spread to his lung, vocal cords, and then his brain. The loss of her father greatly impacted Raye Dawn. Raye Dawn always had a reputation for being a little wild, but after her father's death, many felt she started drinking too much.

Raye Dawn was arrested in April, 2004, just days after her father's funeral, for Actual Physical Control (APC) of a motor vehicle while intoxicated. An APC is when a person is in an operable vehicle with a blood alcohol concentration (BAC) above the legal limit.

It was late night and into early the next morning, shortly after her father's funeral that Raye Dawn, drunk and depressed, pulled over to sleep in her car by the Meeker Apartments. The police came by and noticed a drunken Raye Dawn sleeping in her car. She was then arrested. She was stopped again a few months later while intoxicated, but the officer let her go.

Lance's early childhood was met with tragedy and uncertainty. It's common knowledge among family members that Lance's father, Kevin

Robinson, killed himself on Christmas Day, 1984. On that day, Kevin was supposed to have gotten Lance and his sister for his Christmas visitation. Lance's mother, Kathie Briggs, would not allow him to take the children, and according to the family, he shot himself in the head.

When Lance was a small child, Kathie showed up with her children on the courthouse steps in Pottawat-tamie County and said that she could no longer take care of her children. They were taken into DHS custody.

> **Kathie showed up with her children on the courthouse steps in Pottawattamie County and said that she could no longer take care of her children.**

According to a worker at the time, she used to give Kathie gas money and rides to visitation so that her parental rights would not be terminated. Kathie claims to be a success story of the system. However, it took her almost two years to complete her treatment plan and have her children returned. I have always found it ironic that the system Lance is suing for 15 million dollars, and for changes to the system, is the same system that provided for his care all those years ago.

Evidently, Lance and Raye Dawn grew up in two completely different worlds, though in the same small town. Raye Dawn was young, impulsive, and wild, while Lance had a history of run-ins with the law, from what some have called problems with substance abuse and anger management.

Throughout the early problems, the couple stayed together and was expecting their first child before they married on July 15, 2000. According to witnesses, less than a month before their marriage Lance and Raye Dawn had a physical altercation and she fell backward on the bed.

Following this physical altercation, Raye Dawn suffered from cramps and bleeding. Shortly thereafter, she was rushed to Mission Hill Hospital in Shawnee, Oklahoma where it was discovered the baby had been detached from the uterus. It appears that Raye Dawn and Lance's first child died as a result of of a miscarriage, and it seemed that more misery would follow.

According to the family, Lance sought treatment for his self-destructive issues, and the couple wed on July 15, 2000, when Raye Dawn was 20 and Lance was 22. The marriage was short-lived, as the couple divorced in July, 2002. At the time of their divorce, Raye Dawn had no idea she was pregnant with Kelsey.

Following is a short synopsis of a few of Lance's run-ins with the law from May, 2001, to the end of 2002.

On May 4, 2001, Lance Briggs was arrested for slamming Raye Dawn against the wall with his forearm and holding her there by her throat.

On October 2, 2001, Lance entered a plea to the assault and battery domestic abuse charge. He was ordered to attend anger management, pay a fine, pay a fee to the victim's compensation account (VCA), plus court costs.

On May 30, 2002, Lance broke into Raye Dawn's residence, moved several things around, and according to witnesses, left a note that said, "You want to play games? You decide." The police flagged down Lance as he drove past Raye Dawn's residence with his music blaring. Lance admitted to having broken into Raye Dawn's house, but denied leaving the note. Because the sheriff's office could not locate Raye Dawn's Protective Order against Lance, he was let go by the police.

Again, on July 3, 2002, Raye Dawn's house was broken into. Assistant Chief of Police, Byers, investigated and found the bathroom mirror broken, cabinets and drawers in the kitchen and bedroom open, dug through, and strung about. A window had been the point of entry, and was broken out with the screen pushed in and plastic covering sliced.

Officer Byers located Raye Dawn, who told him that she was staying at her parent's house because her house had a gas leak. When advised of what had happened, Raye Dawn told Officer Byers that she felt Lance was responsible because he had called her just hours before extremely intoxicated, in an attempt to reconcile their pending divorce.

Another reason Raye Dawn felt it was Lance was because the items taken from her home were personal items. She provided the police a list of the missing items that included a carousel horse, flowers, a ceramic swan, a blue porcelain doll, and school yearbooks, as well as several phone messages left by Lance, and a dry erase board that had been found outside with the following message scrolled on it:

"Baby Doll, where are you? I've been calling around for you. I'm worried. Hopefully, I'll find you soon. Me."

It was now August 2, 2002, and the Meeker police responded to an automobile accident. The driver at fault was Lance Briggs. In the other vehicle there were two people who had been injured in the accident. When the police arrived, Lance became extremely verbally abusive and used profanity against the female officer. He directly cussed the female officer several times during this incident. He was also verbally abusive to his mother, and used extreme profanity in the presence of two young children she had with her, when she arrived on the scene.

Even though Lance had the smell of alcohol on his breath, and there was no insurance on the vehicle he was driving, the police let Lance go with his step-father, Royce Briggs.

Finally, on November 9, 2002, Lance was stopped for speeding by Sergeant Leabo. During the traffic stop, Sergeant Leabo learned an arrest warrant had been issued for Lance because of his failure to pay traffic tickets. When Sergeant Leabo arrested him, Lance became verbally abusive toward the officer. As Sergeant Leabo was transporting Lance to the sheriff's office, Lance threatened to harm, not only the officer, but his family as well.

Lance and Raye Dawn Tie a Loose Knot

It was clear that Lance was out of control. Things got so bad that Raye Dawn filed a Petition for a Protective Order at the Lincoln County Courthouse on August 2, 2002, stating, "(Lance) followed me around town on my lunch break. Told me to pull over and then at 12:30 was waiting on me outside my work and told me he could explain. Then when I ignored him, he told me it was going to get worse. Then I went inside and called the cops. He has done this kind of thing and has hurt me before. He has been ordered to stay away from me. He was seen later coming from my home with a boat." Raye Dawn was persuaded to not show up at the hearing, and the protective order was dismissed.

Shortly after Kelsey was born Raye Dawn went home from the hospital, with a newborn in her arms, to care for her dying father so her mother could return to work. When Kelsey was around one-year-old, Raye Dawn returned to work and attended classes at a local college. She and her mother, Gayla, established a routine in which they took turns making sure her father's needs were met during the day while both women worked. Raye Dawn would take Kelsey to daycare each morning, go to work, and go to school. On the nights she didn't have school she would take over for her mother. This went on for about a year with constant work, studying, and struggle.

> Allegedly, Kathie told Raye Dawn, at one point, that Ashley said that she and Lance would not have their own children; instead, they would just keep Kelsey. This is but one example of the contributing factors creating the animosity between the families.

Raye Dawn remained single and several months passed before DHS became involved as a custody battle ensued between the Smith and the

Briggs families. On June 14, 2003, Lance Briggs, 25, had married Ashley Lytle, 19, when she was just one year out of high school.

Allegedly, Kathie told Raye Dawn, at one point, that Ashley said that she and Lance would not have their own children; instead, they would just keep Kelsey. This is but one example of the contributing factors creating the animosity between the families.

Ashley put a poem in her employer's newsletter that clearly showed her love for Kelsey. During this brutal custody case I did not question Ashley's love for Kelsey. Following is Ashley's poem:

"Daddy Come Home?"

The day started out beautifully the morning air humid, the sun barely peeking over the sleepy clouds. The car was packed full of Army gear and gifts from family and friends. I had to face and bare the difficult task of delivering my newly wed husband to Fort Leonard Wood. We started our lives together on June 14, 2003, and I remember agreeing to the terms "for better or for worse." But I don't remember agreeing to see him off to war. My heart was heavy that day: we spent every moment looking deep into each other's eyes and cuddling with our baby girl. We used cameras to capture images but I remember trying to burn the image of his face deep into my memory never wanting to forget. I wanted to keep it safe and hold on to it. My biggest fear is what this is doing to our little girl; she is learning words that she would not normally know until late years.

She asks, "Daddy at?"

"Remember, Daddy in the Army," I tell her.

"Oh, Daddy Army," she replies with a sad look in her eyes.

She will have a new understanding of "he is protecting us." The question that takes my breath away is "Daddy come home?" She is my jewel and the reason I can continue on. So, wives and moms that are alone, continue to be brave, keep the faith, we have a lot to be thankful for.

Ashley Briggs, Customer Service Representative

Ashley was clearly committed to Lance and wanted Kelsey as her own daughter. However, neither family was about to give up without a fight.

Sometime in the fall of 2004, Raye Dawn began dating Michael Porter. It was a whirlwind romance, and they married just months after meeting on April 18, 2005. Michael, 25, was one year younger than Raye Dawn, 26, at the time of their wedding. He was the President of Midwest Industries, his family owned business in located in Shawnee, Oklahoma.

Raye Dawn saw Porter as a "knight in shining armor" amidst all of the turmoil that had been surrounding her life. He appeared to be supportive of her as the pressure from the Briggs family was mounting. The Briggs wanted Ashley to have visitation with Kelsey when Lance was away on active military duty. Raye Dawn refused to allow Ashley to have visitation with a child when her biological father was not home. It is like each time an incident happened, the hatred grew like throwing a dry cedar tree on a brush fire.

Afterthought

It is clear from just these police reports that Lance had a long-running history with the Meeker Police Department. Perhaps Lance's own history caused the officers to be biased against him in Kelsey's case. Is it possible that Kathie would later choose not to tell where Lance was during the custody hearings, for fear that I would find out about his checkered past? *If people want a court to make the best decision, they must be forthcoming and honest with the court regarding their past histories.*

A Deadly Game of Tug of War

CHAPTER FOUR

December 28, 2002
Kelsey Shelton Smith – Born to Two Families That Would NEVER Act as One

On December 28, 2002, Kelsey Shelton Smith, now known as Kelsey Smith-Briggs, was born to Raye Dawn Smith and Lance Briggs, whose birth name was Robinson. (Lance changed his name to Briggs shortly before his marriage to Raye Dawn.)

Kelsey came into this world as a pure-hearted bundle of joy. Born to parents that divorced before her birth and whose families could not share her love with each other.

It was apparent to anyone paying attention that the tug-of-war for little Kelsey had already started at birth. Dual announcements were sent to the local, small town paper by the maternal and paternal sides of Kelsey's family, each giving a different spin to the joyful news, and reflecting the bad blood that existed between the families. Can you imagine two families that could not put everyone's name on the same birth announcement?

> The dual birth announcements reflected the bad blood that existed between the maternal and paternal families.

From reading the birth announcement headlines, readers had no clue the announcements were trumpeting the arrival of the same child. Lance demanded a paternity test after Raye Dawn refused to put his name on the birth certificate. The paternity test had shown that Lance Briggs was indeed Kelsey's father. Kelsey's legal name at the time of the announcement was Kelsey Shelton Smith. Yet, the baby announcement placed in the *Meeker News* by the paternal grandparents in early 2003 read "Baby Girl Briggs." The Briggs' announcement read as follows:

"Baby Girl Briggs –

Royce and Kathie Briggs of Meeker would like to announce the birth of their granddaughter. Kelsey was born at Presbyterian Hospital on December 28, 2002. She weighed 7 pounds.

Her parents are Lance Briggs of Shawnee and Raye Dawn Smith of Meeker." The announcement went on to list numerous Briggs family members.

The Smith family noticed omissions in the first announcement, and Kelsey's name had not yet been legally changed to Briggs. Apparently, this prompted the Smiths to submit their own announcement with the heading of "Baby Girl Smith" in the *Meeker News* on April 24, 2003. The Smith's announcement read as follows:

"Baby Girl Smith – (This announcement boasted a picture of a smiling, happy Kelsey with a full head of black hair.)

Ray and Gayla Smith of Meeker would like to announce the birth of their granddaughter. Kelsey was born at OU Medical Center Presbyterian Tower Hospital on December 28, 2002 at 10:00 P.M. She weighed 7 pounds and was 19" long.

Her parents are Raye Dawn Smith of Meeker and Lance Briggs of Shawnee." This announcement went on to list various members of both the Briggs and Smith families.

Afterthought

At the time of Kelsey's birth, her parents were obviously no longer together. As a result of their prior history, including domestic and substance abuse, Kelsey was born into a broken home, and destined to be raised in conflict.

A Deadly Game of Tug of War

CHAPTER FIVE

Fall '04 Visitation Hearing Devoid ANY Allegations of Abuse

At one point, Lance Briggs, Kelsey's biological father, had been given restricted visitation by the court. Yet, after another court battle, on April 20, 2004, Lance was granted standard visitation with Kelsey. At this point, he was already in arrearage on child support in the amount of $1,001.75. It was at this time that Kelsey's name was officially changed to Kelsey Smith-Briggs, approximately one year after the birth announcement for "Kelsey Briggs."

Initially, Kathie Briggs, Kelsey's paternal grandmother, petitioned for grandparental visitation rights in September of 2004, because Raye Dawn refused to give Lance's visitation rights to Ashley while Lance was away on military duty. Once again, the parties could not resolve an issue involving Kelsey without court involvement.

> At this visitation hearing, there were NO allegations of abuse against Raye Dawn.

At this visitation hearing, there were NO allegations of abuse against Raye Dawn. This hearing was regarding visitation rights only, with absolutely no charges of abuse or neglect. Kathie simply asked that she be granted the visitation that Lance would have exercised if he was home, and not away on active military duty.

I was told Lance would soon be away due to military obligations, so I awarded Lance's visitation to his mother, Kathie, and she began having unsupervised visitation with Kelsey every other weekend. Raye Dawn was trying to keep Kelsey away from Ashley, but Kathie would regularly let Kelsey go with "Mommy" Ashley.

Afterthought

In September, 2004, this hearing appeared to be just a simple visitation hearing, where Raye Dawn had no problem with Kathie seeing Kelsey, but the fight was over how often. I had no idea of the battle that would soon follow involving these two families.

CHAPTER SIX

The Timeline Begins - January, 2005
The Battle Heats Up as DHS Becomes Involved

Though the tug-of-war for Kelsey Smith-Briggs had started at the time of her birth, and continued to smolder through December, 2004, things started to really heat up in January, 2005. At this point, Kelsey was two years old, and the Department of Human Services became involved in the battle.

During 2004, following Raye Dawn's father's death, Kathie seemed to be overly nice to Raye Dawn. She had picked up Kelsey the day Raye Dawn's father died and kept her during the funeral. According to witnesses, Kathie was very supportive during that time and did not appear to be worried about Raye Dawn's ability as a mother. But that soon changed…

It was now January 14, 2005 and Raye Dawn had dropped Kelsey off at a meeting place with the paternal grandmother, Kathie Briggs.

According to Kathie, January 8, 2005, was her regularly scheduled weekend. But when she went to the meeting place to pick up the child, Raye Dawn didn't show. Kathie made phone calls and tried to contact her, but couldn't reach Raye Dawn or find Kelsey. She returned to the meeting place at 6pm a week later, on the 14th, just to see if Raye Dawn would show.

Raye Dawn showed up with Kelsey and told Kathie that she had mixed up the weekends, because of the holidays, and handed Kelsey to Kathie.

Raye Dawn informed Kathie that Kelsey had fallen out of her crib at around 2 or 3am on the 9th and had broken her clavicle (collarbone). Raye Dawn said she was in the bathroom and Kelsey came in whining and saying she wanted out. Kelsey had a history of climbing out of her bed from an early age. Raye Dawn didn't realize Kelsey was injured at the time, so she put Kelsey in bed with her and went back to sleep. The next day she had to work so she took Kelsey to her grandmother's home (Mildred Fowler). According to Mildred, Kelsey played normally. Raye Dawn said she didn't notice anything was wrong either until she saw some swelling on her collarbone. Later that day, when she realized Kelsey was hurt, she took her to the emergency room that same day. Kelsey was diagnosed with a broken clavicle (collarbone) and the ER doctor noted scratches to Kelsey's neck and arms. Kelsey was given a brace for her collarbone and Tylenol for pain.

When Raye Dawn dropped Kelsey off with Kathie on January 14, 2005, it was dark. Kelsey, as Kathie described, was lethargic as she laid her head on Kathie's shoulder. Kathie stated that she just put Kelsey in the car and drove her home without really looking at her. Once she got home, she noticed bruising on both sides of her face.

Kathie's son, and father of Kelsey, Lance Briggs, along with his wife, Ashley, came to Kathie's home for a birthday party that evening. They stayed about an hour and then took Kelsey with them to Ashley's mom's home. By Kathie's estimated timeline, it was around 30 minutes later, as Ashley was giving Kelsey her bath, that she noticed the bruising on Kelsey's buttocks.

Allegedly, Lance and Ashley decided to take Kelsey to the emergency room at the Shawnee hospital at around 10pm to be checked out for signs of abuse. No one called Raye Dawn, but they did call Kathie Briggs, and she met them there.

The Meeker police were notified by hospital personnel that a toddler from the Meeker area, possibly suffering from child abuse, was being examined at the hospital. The police began by questioning the doctor and paternal family members. According to Kathie, Sergeant Carl Leabo asked her if she was "prepared to raise a grandchild." He also allegedly said the child would never leave her arms because he would call DHS and they would give Kelsey to her because she was the natural grandmother.

When Sergeant Leabo was later asked about this statement, he stated that he didn't recall making those comments. He said it was probably something more along the lines of if this case comes out worse, where I have to seize the child, would you take the child? He further stated he wouldn't have had the authority to tell Kathie that Kelsey would never leave her arms.

Kathie further claimed that Sergeant Leabo advised her to take emergency custody of the child and not return her to the mother at 6pm on Sunday night, as was their regular routine.

The police report shows the emergency room doctor stated that the injuries on Kelsey weren't consistent with Raye Dawn's version of Kelsey falling out of her crib. The police continued their investigation Saturday, January 15, 2005, and visited Raye Dawn's apartment and questioned her. Assistant Chief Byers and Sergeant Leabo conducted their interview of Raye Dawn and inspected her apartment. They were shown the bed Kelsey fell from and a plastic toddler slide beside the bed that was possibly where Kelsey hit her face, causing the bruising. After interviewing hospital personnel, the Briggs, and Raye Dawn, and inspecting Raye Dawn's apartment, the police ruled the injuries as accidental.

In his report, Officer Byers made statements regarding Raye Dawn's apartment, "Toys strung out…but the apartment as a whole was clean, well-kept, nothing strung out, no dirty dishes, no trash lying around. It was a well-kept apartment." He further stated he had seen a hairbrush lying on the floor in Kelsey's bedroom. Both officers concluded that it was plausible that Kelsey fell on the brush while running through the house, causing the marks on her buttocks, rather than Raye Dawn purposely abusing the child.

Both Sergeant Leabo and Officer Byers found Raye Dawn to be "open and truthful, not deceptive or trying to hide anything." Raye Dawn told the police that she didn't even know there was bruising on Kelsey's buttocks; that was new information to her. She had also kept pictures and detailed logs of conversations she'd had with Lance and his family members because of her fear that something may happen to her child because of Lance's history of abuse. The officers found it odd she would keep such detailed records. In the usual course of their investigations, this was not common for someone who would abuse their own child.

At the guardianship trial in February, 2005, both the Meeker police officers and DHS investigators testified that the broken collarbone and facial bruises were not child abuse, but accidental injuries. The police officers' opinion differed from DHS's on the bruised buttocks. DHS saw the bruising as possible abuse, whereas the police officers *did not* believe the bruises were from abuse.

The police officers also noted that Raye Dawn had pictures of bruising she had seen on Kelsey when she got her back from visitation with Lance. Many of the photos did not have a date and therefore could not be used by the officers to further their investigation.

The Briggs alleged that Raye Dawn had a serious alcohol problem. Many considered Raye Dawn to be a party animal and believed she had been intoxicated when Kelsey was injured.

At the February, 2005 guardianship hearing, some of Raye Dawn's own family alleged they saw her buy beer shortly after her father's funeral. Officer Byers also admitted to pulling over Raye Dawn at a later date in 2004 when she had been drinking. She was a short distance from home and Officer Byers let her go without arresting her.

The Briggs family felt that from the time Raye Dawn was arrested and charged with Actual Physical Control of a motor vehicle while intoxicated (APC), in April, 2004, her drinking had spun out of control, and she may have taken out her anger on Kelsey and spanked her with a hair brush.

However, neither of the officers believed that Raye Dawn's history of drinking had anything to do with the possible abuse charges. They had asked if she had a drinking problem and she told them there was no problem. Did Raye Dawn have a drinking problem that affected the outcome of this case? All of the classes required to be completed under the DHS Individualized Treatment Plan showed a low likelihood of an alcohol and drug abuse problem. *Did the mental health professionals miss something in their testing of Raye Dawn?*

On Sunday, January 16, 2005, Kathie refused to return Kelsey to Raye Dawn because of abuse allegations. When Kathie refused to return Kelsey, Raye Dawn went to the Meeker police. An officer called Kathie and informed her that Raye Dawn was prepared to file child abduction charges against her if she did not return Kelsey. Kathie told the police officer that she would call DHS if they attempted to force her to return Kelsey. Raye Dawn was scared of Kelsey becoming part of the system, so she allowed Kathie to keep Kelsey one more day.

Kathie would return Kelsey to Raye Dawn on Monday, January, 17, 2005, at 2pm. It was one week later, January, 24, 2005, when Kathie showed up in my chambers with her attorney. She was granted emergency temporary custody of Kelsey, based on the information Kathie and her attorney provided to me.

Once Kathie received guardianship, DHS continued their investigation. An investigator with the Department of Human Services checked out Kelsey's injuries and interviewed Raye Dawn, her mother Gayla Smith, her grandmother Mildred Fowler, and then Kathie Briggs and Lance Briggs.

Initially, the DHS investigator was concerned that there may have been some kind of abuse occurring because of the injuries to Kelsey's buttocks, the upper part of her back, the lower part of her upper thigh, and her face. The bruising on Kelsey's buttocks was a series of small spots, consistent with possibly a hairbrush striking her. The DHS worker didn't think this injury was consistent with a child falling from her crib. She noted that Raye Dawn had no idea where the bruises came from because she had spent the previous night at her mother's home with Kelsey, and then had taken Kelsey to daycare, where she spent the entire day. Raye Dawn only had her for one hour before giving her to Kathie. Once Kelsey was given to Kathie, she, along with Lance, had Kelsey for a period of approximately four hours before the bruises were "discovered."

Everyone that took care of Kelsey that week denied seeing the bruises on Kelsey's buttocks. It was said to have been impossible for the bruising to have occurred between the hours of 6pm and 11pm when the picture was taken, but could they have occurred from the hours of 5pm to 6pm while Raye Dawn had Kelsey? When Kelsey was returned to Raye Dawn the following week, the bruises were gone.

In her investigation, the DHS investigator asked Lance Briggs if he had a history of domestic abuse and he said no, that he'd never abused anyone. At that point, DHS had no reason to believe that the abuse had been perpetrated by the Briggs family and did not verify Lance's denial of having a history of domestic abuse. They also were not able to pull up the information about Kathie previously giving up her children to DHS.

On January 21, 2005, Raye Dawn took Kelsey to see a doctor to have blood tests performed in an effort to explain why the child bruised so easily. To this day, I have never seen the results of those tests.

On January 24, 2005, Royce and Kathie Briggs petitioned the court to be guardians over Kelsey. As part of their petition, they asked to be granted emergency temporary custody of Kelsey. I granted their request on January 24, 2005, and Kelsey was placed in their custody until further hearing on February, 4, 2005.

When DHS interviewed Raye Dawn after Kelsey was given to Kathie on January 24, 2005 she cried uncontrollably. It was apparent Raye Dawn was devastated by the abuse charges and loss of Kelsey. Raye Dawn was willing to do whatever it took to prove she wanted her daughter back in her care and custody.

The ultimate findings from the DHS reports showed that Kelsey's bruising on her buttocks had been caused by abuse. At that time, all signs pointed to Raye Dawn. While the police had dismissed any abuse allegations, DHS didn't want to take any chances and leave Kelsey with Raye Dawn until it was figured out exactly what was taking place. In addition, DHS wanted Raye Dawn to complete certain classes before Kelsey was returned.

Afterthought

According to witnesses, Kelsey was at her great-grandmother Mildred's during the day on Monday, January 10, 2005, and Tuesday, January 11, 2005, and with Raye Dawn at night. Raye Dawn had Kelsey all Wednesday, January 12, 2005, and then they spent the night with Gayla Thursday, January 13, 2005. Raye Dawn took Kelsey to daycare Friday morning, January 14, 2005, and then picked her up from there at 5pm. She then took her to Kathie Briggs at 6pm.

If Raye Dawn caused the bruises on Kelsey's buttocks, when could she have done it? Kelsey was with Mildred the first part of the week and with both Raye Dawn and Gayla toward the end of the week. This timeline has always caused me to wonder if Raye Dawn could have caused the bruises. The only times, according to witnesses, that Raye Dawn was alone with Kelsey during that week was on Wednesday, and during the one hour timeframe she had her on Friday. Since Kelsey was still in diapers, if Raye Dawn had abused Kelsey on Wednesday, either Gayla or Julie, the daycare owner, would have seen the bruises.

Raye Dawn said the fresh bruises found on Kelsey by the Briggs were something new to her. Could the policemen's speculation of Kelsey falling on the brush while running through the home have been the actual culprit? Could that four-hour time span when Kelsey was in the custody of Kathie, Lance, and Ashley have resulted in fresh injuries? Could this all have been planned to take custody away from Raye Dawn? Did Raye Dawn, in fact, commit the abuse during the one hour timeframe that she had Kelsey when she picked her up from daycare until she delivered her to Kathie? Did someone else abuse Kelsey? The answers to these questions are still being sought in court and in the media to this day.

CHAPTER SEVEN

The Custody Battle of February 4, 2005

It was Friday, February 4, 2005 when Kelsey's life was involved in yet another court battle. The paternal grandparents, Royce and Kathie Briggs, had requested an emergency hearing to obtain full legal custody of two-year-old Kelsey. A local attorney represented the Petitioners, Royce and Kathie Briggs as they claimed that the mother, Raye Dawn Smith, had abused her child after Kelsey broke her collarbone while climbing out of bed.

The abuse charges were filed when Kathie had turned to DHS after the police dropped their child abuse investigation of Raye Dawn. Kathie's main issue in the case was Kelsey's broken collarbone. She didn't believe that Kelsey could have possibly sustained the injury when climbing out of bed and falling onto a plastic slide.

Kathie had emergency temporary guardianship of Kelsey, but according to Kathie, Kelsey stayed with Lance and Ashley Briggs the night before the hearing, and had been with them two nights before that as well. During that time, Kathie allowed Lance to see Kelsey, but she refused to allow Raye Dawn visitation.

Kathie worried for Kelsey's safety while in Raye Dawn's care, but not in Lance's, even though Kathie admitted that Lance had one charge of domestic abuse against him. She claimed she had no knowledge of him ever abusing Raye Dawn. During the proceedings, she completely downplayed Lance's problems.

Initially, I appointed Sheila Kirk, a local attorney, who would later be my opponent in the 2006 re-election campaign to represent Kelsey. I knew Sheila was from Meeker, and would possibly know the dynamics of the people involved in this case. Sheila came to me and requested to not be assigned to the case, because she previously represented Raye Dawn in her divorce against Lance Briggs. Once Sheila withdrew, I appointed another attorney as guardian ad litem, for Kelsey.

Greg Wilson, an attorney from Shawnee, Oklahoma, represented Kelsey's mother, Raye Dawn Smith.

The courtroom was full of people, who were mostly there to support Raye Dawn. I recognized some of the faces of her supporters as good, solid citizens. I could not understand what had moved that many people to show up for this hearing. I guess it was clear that the battle for Kelsey had spread beyond the families.

Among Raye Dawn's supporters who testified that day was Mildred, Raye Dawn's grandmother and Kelsey's great-grandmother. She spoke about Kelsey's broken collarbone. According to Mildred, she had seen bruising on Kelsey's face that would have been consistent with the fall from Kelsey's bed and possibly onto the slide.

The day after Kelsey went to the doctor for her collarbone, Kelsey stayed at Mildred's home while Raye Dawn attended college classes. Mildred fell asleep with Kelsey on the couch while patting her leg. When they woke up, Mildred noticed there were four red spots where her hand had been on Kelsey's leg. Since the start of the abuse allegations by the Briggs family, she worried that because Kelsey bruised so easily and had marks on her after a simple patting of the leg that someone may think that she spanked Kelsey, according to her, she had never spanked Kelsey in her life.

The Briggs family members have said terrible things about Mildred. The first time I personally met Mildred was a few months after Kelsey's death. I'll never forget Mildred walking up to me at the 7th grade basketball game in Chandler where she was watching her great-granddaughter play basketball. I did not recognize her at first, because I had only seen her in the courtroom setting.

She approached me and asked if I was Judge Key, and I responded, "Yes, Ma'am." With a little tear in her eye, she apologized for what the media was doing to me and how she knew the twisted facts had to be taking a toll on me. She reached out, took my hand, looked me square in the eye, and told me she was praying for me. I wrestled with Mildred's statement all that night. How could this sweet, elderly lady be praying for me after all she had been through since the beginning of the custody battle and ultimately Kelsey's death?

If I had broken the law, as Kathie claims, or had done something wrong in this case that contributed to Kelsey's death, shouldn't the maternal family be upset with me too? In my opinion, Mildred's graciousness toward me in her time of grief displayed her Christian values and true character.

The most independent supporter of Raye Dawn's to testify at the February 4th hearing was Julie, the owner of Kelsey's in-home daycare. She had taken care of Kelsey since before her first birthday until the battle for the little girl turned ugly. Prior to this time period, she did not know anyone involved in this case, yet at one point, she had to order Kathie Briggs never to return to her home.

According to Julie, when Kelsey first started with her daycare, she was a funny and busy kid. Kelsey was very active and climbed on everything. Julie couldn't even place Kelsey in a portable crib for naptime, because she would climb out. Instead, she had to be placed on the couch or on a mat on the floor.

From Julie's observations, Raye Dawn was a good mother and had always been appropriate with her daughter. When Julie started noticing bruises on Kelsey in August of 2004, she wasn't overly concerned. Kelsey was very active, fair skinned, seemed to fall down a lot, and bruised easily. However, when the bruising became more consistent, she became alarmed.

According to Julie's observations, in late August to early September, 2004, around the same time Kathie Briggs was granted grandparent visitation, Kelsey had a couple of bruises on her upper leg. In October, 2004, she had one on her arm and one on her upper thigh by her buttocks. As was Julie's custom, she called the DHS daycare licensing supervisor and reported the increased occurrences of bruising. DHS told her to keep track of who Kelsey had been with at the time she noticed any bruising.

At the direction of DHS, Julie made notes that the bruises would show up on Mondays after Kelsey had visited Lance and Ashley, or Kathie Briggs for the weekend. This concerned her because she hadn't noticed bruises on Kelsey before Kathie's weekend visitation had been awarded.

Julie contacted Raye Dawn about her concerns and asked if she noticed the bruises. Raye Dawn confirmed that she had seen them. According to Julie, Raye Dawn was also concerned, because when Kelsey returned home after one visit with the Briggs, she thought some of the bruises were slashes like finger marks over Kelsey's knees, and some looked like finger marks on her buttocks.

In January, 2005, after Kathie got the emergency guardianship custody order, she went to pick Kelsey up from Julie's home daycare. According to Julie, Kathie jumped out of her car, instantly became angry, and started yelling at her. Julie held on to Kelsey as Kathie grabbed her little arm and tried to rip her loose. Julie was afraid that Kathie would hurt Kelsey by pulling on her in that manner, so she let Kathie take little Kelsey.

Once Kathie snatched Kelsey from Julie's arms, Julie told Kathie that she was not to come back to her property. Julie felt that because she ran an in-home daycare and other children she cared for were present, they did not need to witness Kathie yelling and screaming at their caretaker.

As Kathie angrily stormed off, she informed Julie that Kelsey would not be returning to her daycare and Julie could feel free to fill Kelsey's spot.

I always found it interesting that according to Julie, Kelsey did not hold her arms out to Kathie or act like she wanted to go with her. Julie came to the hearing to support Raye Dawn because she had seen, first hand, Kelsey's reaction to Kathie. Raye Dawn seemed so small sitting near her attorney with her countless other supporters behind her. She was absolutely tiny at probably no more than 5' tall with a very slight build.

However, her confidence came through as she took the witness stand. At times, during her testimony, I felt that she came across as whiny and complaining. Her words were very matter-of-fact. It was clear to me that she came to fight for the return of her child.

As she spoke, she leaned forward into the microphone with her elbows resting on the arms of the chair. She locked her finger together in front of her and never took her eyes off of the attorneys as they asked her questions. There was nothing deceptive or defensive about her testimony.

As a result of the abuse allegations, Raye Dawn had taken Kelsey to the doctor in order to check for a blood deficiency that would explain why she bruised so easily. I have, to this day, never seen the results of those tests. However, I know the test that DHS did months later for brittle bone disease was inconclusive. The OU Medical Center wanted to do further testing, but the request was denied by DHS, because it was not cost effective.

Before any abuse allegations were made against Raye Dawn, she took pictures after Kelsey's visit with Kathie on January 1, 2005. At that visit, Lance had been present. Kelsey came home with marks around her knees that resembled fingers and four finger-sized bruises around her arm. Raye Dawn did not bring these bruises to Lance or Kathie's attention because she did not have a good relationship with them. She did not feel they could discuss anything without yelling, screaming, or accusing each other of causing the marks on Kelsey.

Raye Dawn admitted her form of discipline included occasionally spanking Kelsey with a pat on the diaper or a spat on her hands. Raye Dawn said this form of punishment was what she received as a child, and therefore, it was how she was raising Kelsey. Raye Dawn claimed that she had never left a mark on Kelsey when spanking her.

Raye Dawn, however, worried that Lance would take out his anger on Kelsey while in Kathie's care. She alleged that during their marriage, Lance had reared back and punched her in the face. His temper was so out of control during the time the couple separated that he broke into Raye Dawn's home, trashed it, and threw her stuff in a pond. Raye Dawn was terrified of Lance, so she went to stay with her parents and slept between her mother and dying father for protection. According to Meeker police reports, which substantiate Raye Dawn's claims, Lance's actions led him to be charged with domestic abuse. Raye Dawn spoke openly and honestly about the problems that she and Lance had during their relationship.

On the other hand, Kathie Briggs' answers to questions asked were defensive, short, and the only time she elaborated was when she was defending Lance. She sat back in her chair and seemed to struggle for answers, specifically when the questions involved her son, Lance, of whom she was notably protective. Kathie seemed to be in her late 40s, short, medium build.

Her husband, Royce Briggs was tall with a slender build. He seemed very quiet, as someone who thinks before he speaks. He sat at the counsel table most of the time with his shoulder against the wall. Royce is someone that I would like to have a conversation with regarding this matter. I have felt drawn to him before when we have run into each other in public. However, with all that has happened, and the negative way that Kathie has portrayed my role in this case, I have never approached him when I've seen him at events.

On the side of the Briggs family was Ashley Briggs, Lance's young wife. She barely looked 18. It has always puzzled me how someone so young was able to emotionally handle the mess into which she had married. She was coping with Lance and his military obligation, along with the custody battle over Kelsey.

Lance, the biological father of Kelsey, was not present at this, or any other hearing regarding his daughter's welfare.

According to Kathie, Lance was stationed in Fort Leonard Wood, Missouri, but had returned to take care of his medical leave. He had been home the morning of this hearing, but left early to return to Missouri. Kathie said he was home on Veteran's Day, Thanksgiving, Christmas, and Martin Luther King's birthday. According to Kathie, Lance had to return to Missouri to finish moving his belongings. I have always wondered why Lance didn't make arrangements to stay for the hearing. In all of my dealings with the military, a GI can make arrangements to be at a hearing involving his child if there are abuse allegations.

> Lance, the biological father of Kelsey, was not present at this, or any other hearing regarding his daughter's welfare.

Representatives and investigators from DHS were also present and testified at this hearing. According to an investigator for DHS, the child abuse case was still being investigated. I was informed that if custody wasn't taken away from Raye Dawn, DHS would ask me to place Kelsey into their custody. The DHS worker did not believe that the various colors of bruises on Kelsey's body had been caused by an accidental fall. At the time of her investigation, she had no knowledge of Lance history of domestic abuse or Kathie's history of child abandonment. The investigator had not looked into the possibility that some of the injuries may have occurred during the four hours that Kathie and Lance had Kelsey. DHS assumed the bruising had been caused by Raye Dawn, though the Meeker Police Department did not concur with their conclusion.

Assistant Chief of Police, Matt Byers, a man in his early 30s, slender build, medium height, and close cropped hair, and Sergeant Carl Leabo, late 40s, tall with grey hair, of the Meeker Police Department concluded from their investigation that nothing was found to cause them to think that Kelsey had been abused. As far as the Meeker Police Department was concerned, the investigation of abuse was closed.

Because Office Byers and Sergeant Leabo concluded that Kelsey's bruising to her buttocks was an accidental injury, they have been widely criticized by the media. I have always felt that the criticism of Officer Byers and Sergeant Leabo after Kelsey's death was extremely unfair. Sergeant Leabo has attended several child abuse training seminars for law enforcement officers. At that time, he simply looked at the facts and his prior knowledge of those involved and made his best decision. Officer Byers is a well-respected law enforcement official. He has worked for the Town of Meeker and at times, has assisted the District Attorney's Drug Task Force.

After Kelsey's death, Officer Byers and I spoke. I'll never forget him telling me that during an interview with Kathie Briggs in January she told him that Mike Porter was a "victim of circumstances" and she was not concerned about him.

Summary

The testimony from each side was polar opposite during the guardianship trial, which made my job that much harder. DHS, the police, and almost everyone agreed the collarbone and facial bruising was the result of an accidental fall. The unresolved issue was the bruising on Kelsey's buttocks. Ultimately, the timeline of events did not clearly indicate the true culprit for this injury, a pattern that continued throughout this sad affair.

However, I was faced with the decision to allow the child to go home with her mother, in which case DHS would step in and ask to take her away, making her a ward of the state, or send her back to the paternal grandparents where she had been in protective custody, but often visiting the home of her young step-mother and her father, who had a history of domestic abuse.

Kelsey had two families who clearly wanted her, so the thought of her being taken away and placed in state custody in a foster home seemed extreme. I felt, at the time, there was no other option but to leave Kelsey where she was, with the Briggs family.

I granted Raye Dawn visitation in the presence of her grandmother, Mildred Fowler, from 6pm the day of court until noon on the following Monday. At this point, the DHS investigator informed me that the DHS investigation would be completed by the following Friday. The custody order was to remain temporary until the following Friday, February 11, 2005.

After the Hearing

On February 11th the parties reappeared and the DA's office asked for more time to file a deprived petition. Therefore, I granted the DA's office 30 days until March 11, 2005, to file a deprived petition. I consolidated the guardianship and deprived case to be heard simultaneously.

On February 23, 2005, the DA's office did file their petition, alleging Kelsey was a deprived child because physical abuse was suspected as evidenced by bruising and abrasions on her buttocks, thigh, lower back, and face.

Afterthought

I felt then and I still feel now the fundamental problem with this case was lack of communication between the families. The participants could not talk to each other regarding the concerns they had with Kelsey's welfare. As in many other cases, it has been shown to be a difficult task to raise a child in a loving, secure environment when the families involved have difficulty speaking or being civil to one another. I ask myself, "What would have happened if these two families had the ability to communicate in a loving, thoughtful way?"

CHAPTER EIGHT

The Impact of the Battle Was Taking Its Toll

When the Department of Human Services finished its investigation, they concluded Raye Dawn had abused Kelsey or allowed it to happen because of the bruises on her buttocks. DHS felt that Raye Dawn had told conflicting stories of the night Kelsey was injured. The DHS worker stated that at one point Raye Dawn had said she was in the bathroom when Kelsey fell out of bed, and to someone else she said she was in bed when Kelsey fell.

Also, the physician did not note the facial bruising the night she was taken in for her broken clavicle. The doctor's notes do show there were scratches to Kelsey's neck and arm. The ER physician on duty, when Lance took Kelsey to the ER, reported the bruises were non-accidental and possibly the result of abuse. The DHS investigator called the ER doctor. During her investigation with the doctor, he said the facial bruising may not have been noticeable at the time he saw Kelsey on the initial visit with Raye Dawn because it was only 14 hours after the fall. When Raye Dawn was allowed to see Kelsey again, the bruises were not on Kelsey, neither were the bruises that had been photographed on her buttocks.

March 11, 2005 Hearing

When we reassembled on March 11, 2005, the Briggs family had guardianship of Kelsey and was complaining about Michael Porter. They were willing to let Raye Dawn have unsupervised visits as long as Porter was not around Kelsey. Before the March hearing, there was little discussion about Michael Porter. This was when the allegations against Porter really started to fly.

At the conclusion of this hearing, I issued a temporary order allowing Raye Dawn to have unsupervised visitation from noon on every Wednesday until noon on Thursday as long as Michael Porter was not in the home at the time of visitation. If Lance was in Oklahoma prior to his deployment to Iraq, he could have visitation, overriding anyone else's scheduled visitation.

I continued the hearing on the guardianship and the deprived petition until June 6, 2005.

After the March 11, 2005 hearing, DHS met Raye Dawn outside the courtroom and informed her of the requirements that would need to be fulfilled in order for Kelsey to be returned to her. She had to complete a Drug and Alcohol Assessment and any follow-up treatment recommended, anger management, and domestic violence classes, along with parenting classes. DHS was advised by Raye Dawn that she would need to call her worker to schedule an appointment for her Strength and Needs Assessment. This assessment involves an interview of the parent by a DHS worker to determine if other courses or classes are needed to improve the home environment once the child is returned. Raye Dawn's Strength and Needs Assessment was completed and it was determined by DHS that no additional classes or assessments were required.

At the March 11, 2005 hearing I continued the case until June 6, 2005 for a hearing on the guardianship and the deprived petition. The temporary order allowed for Raye Dawn to have visitation from noon on every Wednesday until noon on Thursday. If Lance was in Oklahoma prior to his deployment to Iraq, he could have visitation, regardless of whose visitation it was. Raye Dawn's visitation would be unsupervised, as long as Michael Porter wasn't in the home at the time of visitation.

On at least three separate occasions, during the time Kathie had temporary guardianship of Kelsey, she took Kelsey to DHS and Kelsey was asleep and would not wake up for the worker to fully examine her. It has been alleged that Kathie continuously had Kelsey on unnecessary medicines and that Kathie took Kelsey to the doctor repeatedly. DHS workers noted that while in Kathie's custody, Kelsey seemed lethargic and slept most of the time.

On March 24, 2005, Raye Dawn had visitation with Kelsey in her apartment. According to Raye Dawn's interview with DHS, Kelsey was running on the tile floor and looking back to see if Raye Dawn was following when she fell and bruised her nose and right knee. When Kathie got Kelsey back after the visit and noticed the abrasions, she immediately took Kelsey to the emergency room in Shawnee. At the ER someone contacted the statewide abuse hotline and reported the injuries. According to DHS personnel, this was done even though Kathie believed the fall was accidental. She simply wanted it documented for the custody case. Kelsey was examined at the ER and she was fine with just a small abrasion. No prescriptions or other medical treatment was needed and she was not asked to bring Kelsey back for any follow-up exam.

> A red flag was raised for me, as a judge, when DHS told me Kelsey's hair began falling out in clumps while in the care of Kathie Briggs.

Although she was in protective custody, it was apparent that Kelsey wasn't adjusting to being in the Briggs home. A red flag was raised for me, as a judge, when DHS told me Kelsey's hair began falling out in clumps while in the care of Kathie Briggs. Kelsey's hair was falling out to the point that she had a bald spot on the back of her head the size of a baseball. She began self-mutilating by biting her arms, and as clearly stated in Kelsey's obituary submitted by the Briggs, she was apparently biting the Briggs family as well. Kelsey's behavior and hair loss during this time was all documented by DHS.

Pursuant to the instructions of DHS, after discovering Kelsey's deteriorated state, Raye Dawn called her lawyer with her concerns. Marie Larson, who was Greg Wilson's secretary at the time, made an appointment for Kelsey with Dr. Koons for April 4, 2005. The doctor informed Raye Dawn that the hair follicles were not raised so it appeared that the hair had just fallen out and had not been pulled out. The doctor believed the stress of Kelsey being away from her mother was the cause.

Apparently, Raye Dawn attempted to discuss the hair loss issue with Kathie, but she was told that Kathie purchased a doll for Kelsey so that Kelsey could pull out the doll's hair instead of her own.

It was alleged Kelsey also had bruises, scratches, and scrapes after visits with Kathie, but the Smiths did not report them to DHS every time. When Kelsey was seen with a cat scratch across her face, people overheard Kathie tell Raye Dawn, "That's what she gets for sitting on the cat." Anyone who ever saw how active Kelsey was realized this little girl would get bumps, bruised, and scrapes from time to time.

Raye Dawn reported her concerns about the changes in Kelsey to DHS at that time. According to reports, they assumed it was stress. After visitations when it was time for Raye Dawn to return Kelsey to the Briggs, she would cry and cling to her mom and say she didn't like "Mommy Ashley" and she didn't want to see "Kafie."

There were many reports from February, 2005, to June, 2005, of her acting strangely when in the care of Kathie. Kelsey would throw fits, bite, kick, scream, scratch; she just did not appear to be the same child.

Afterthought

Why Kelsey acted differently while in the custody of Kathie Briggs is unclear. Why Kelsey was timid, lethargic, and asleep during almost every DHS visit is also unclear. But what's clear is that the tug-of-war was starting to get to the child both mentally and physically.

One of the ironies in this case is that Marie Larson later dated Lance Briggs. After Marie ended the relationship, Lance was arrested for breaking into her house on July 6, 2006, and dragging her out by her hair. He would later plead to two counts of assault and battery. One was on Miss Larson. The other was on a female friend who was staying at her apartment for Marie's protection due to prior threats by Lance. Once again, Lance is court ordered to attend anger management.

> Once again, Lance is court ordered to attend anger management.

A Deadly Game of Tug of War

CHAPTER NINE

Kelsey Becomes Bruised and Broken

In April, 2005, the Briggs still had temporary guardianship of Kelsey and Raye Dawn had regular visitation. It was during this time, on April 14th, that Kelsey went to the zoo with Raye Dawn's sister-in-law, Miste. She was wearing a pair of pink platform flip flops and had fallen off a raised sidewalk and sprained her ankle.

Out of fear of abuse allegations, Miste and Raye Dawn took Kelsey to the emergency room that day. According to the x-rays and doctor report, there were not any visible fractures at that time. Raye Dawn returned Kelsey back to Kathie that same evening, and picked her up the next day on the 15th. During this time, the doctor had instructed the family to require Kelsey to walk on her injured foot so it would not become stiff. Kelsey walked from the 15th through the 18th while in the care of Raye Dawn, though she favored her injury.

Kathie told DHS that Raye Dawn had returned Kelsey on the 18th of April. At that time, Kelsey took four steps in Wal-Mart and then never walked again while in Kathie's care. Kathie said she thought nothing about Kelsey not walking and just let her crawl around until Raye Dawn picked her up on the 21st.

Raye Dawn reported to DHS that when she picked Kelsey up, all Kelsey did was whimper, crawl, and refuse to walk.

Since Raye Dawn had been told by the doctor to make Kelsey walk on that foot or it would stiffen, she assumed that Kathie did not follow the doctor's orders and that Kelsey's foot had become stiff. Over the weekend, she worked with Kelsey and had her walk.

After Kelsey became progressively worse, Raye Dawn took her to the DHS office on the 25th, where it was noted that her leg was swollen and hot to the touch. At the instruction of DHS, Raye Dawn immediately transported Kelsey from the DHS office to the hospital where Dr. Koons and Dr. Barrett, an orthopedic pediatrician were waiting. It was determined that both of Kelsey's tibias were fractured, but that the injuries occurred at separate times. Her legs were cast and she was sent home with Raye Dawn.

According to Dr. Koons' medical report, the X-rays of Kelsey's tibia showed a non-displaced long spiral fracture on both tibias. A consultation was done with Dr. Barrett, who had noted that the right tibia fracture was consistent with the injury of walking on the flip flops and twisting her ankle, and had occurred in the appropriate timeframe. However, Dr. Barrett felt like the fracture on the left tibia had occurred more recently than the right, and that it could have been caused by Kelsey putting all her weight on the left leg, while compensating for the fracture on her right leg. She said she had seen the same type of fracture the week before. Both of Kelsey's legs were put into casts.

On May 2nd Kathie Briggs took Kelsey to see an orthopedic surgeon at OU Medical Center in Oklahoma City for a second opinion on her broken tibias. According to the doctor's medical report, Kelsey had suffered from bilateral tibia fractures that occurred on separate occasions because they were in different stages of healing. He further stated that the injury occurred by a twist to the leg and that at Kelsey's age a stress fracture could not have occurred. He stated he had never seen bilateral toddler fractures of the tibia as a result of overcompensation.

In his opinion, the finding could be seen as toddler's fractures, but consideration should be made for the possibility that they were from non-accidental trauma.

At this time, the doctor removed the casts from Kelsey's legs and didn't recast them. He said they were not needed.

Raye Dawn took her back to her regular doctor on May 6th and had her legs recast. Without the casts, Kelsey was unable to walk, and Dr. Barrett felt that she needed them in casts so they would heal properly.

Raye Dawn Marries Michael Porter

Raye Dawn told DHS she was unaware of her visitation with Kelsey being restricted. As per my ruling on March 11, 2005, Michael Porter was not to be in the home during her visitation. Since she did not understand this stipulation, she married him on April 18, 2005.

Three days before their marriage ceremony, on April 15, 2005, Michael Porter was visiting a friend and had Kelsey with him. According to Michael, Kelsey fell through a screen door while looking outside at some puppies, which resulted in bruised thighs and bruising to her upper rib cage.

On April 27, 2005, while Kelsey was sleeping with her step-sister, Kelsey was allegedly elbowed in the face, resulting in a purple bruise to her nose that went up to her eyebrow, leaving a knot the size of a quarter by her right eye.

It is unknown if Raye Dawn was still sleeping when Porter went into Kelsey and his daughter's room and found that Kelsey had been injured. DHS was told he woke up his daughter and asked her if she elbowed Kelsey in her sleep. She said that she did not. He then told her that he thought she did because of the bump on Kelsey's nose.

Kelsey's bruises were photographed and documented by DHS on April 29th.

Afterthought

The struggle of power over Kelsey was not limited to these two families. This is clearly evident when one family's doctor placed casts on Kelsey, and the other family's doctor then determined them unnecessary and removed them. After the casts were removed, Kelsey was unable to walk, so the first doctor determined she needed the casts for proper healing, and Kelsey's legs were then recast.

Unfortunately, it is unethical for doctors to compare notes or discuss diagnosis of a patient. Perhaps if there were open communication regarding Kelsey's legs, the tug-of-war would not have caused the child to go through the pain of struggling to walk when her casts were removed before she had time to heal.

Kathie Briggs asked DHS to look at Miste Smith as the perpetrator for abuse, because Kelsey was in her care when her ankle was sprained. DHS did not believe this injury was suspicious until a second opinion was sought by Kathie Briggs.

Looking back, why would someone who took the child to the doctor for minor injuries not take her when she quit walking? It had been widely discussed that Kathie enrolled Kelsey in gymnastics at this same time, but it's unknown as to whether or not she took her to gymnastics while her leg was injured.

What happened to Kelsey's legs? That's a question that is on the minds of the parties involved in this case to this day.

CHAPTER TEN

June, 2005
Kelsey Went Home

The guardianship hearing that took place on June 15 and 16, 2005, has been called into question by the Briggs family and the media. It was at this hearing that I returned Kelsey to her mother, Raye Dawn. There are several aspects of this hearing that have been twisted, misquoted, and in turn, misunderstood by the general public.

I chose not to speak about the case or my decision publicly, because it was inappropriate at the time, given the fact that a child died and two families were grieving. Death threats on my family and against me also compelled me to remain out of the spotlight following these events.

Though I have asked repeatedly for the transcripts from this hearing to be released, so that those who were not present will have a better understanding of my decision and the events, testimony, and evidence that led to my decision, my requests have remained ignored. Therefore, I will share with you the events of this trial, from my perspective, so that you will understand my decision to return Kelsey to her mother.

The amended deprived petition and guardianship action were actually set to be tried on June 6, 2005. A few days prior, the DA had filed a motion to continue (postpone) the case. The parties came to my chambers on that day and advised me they were negotiating a resolution. The negotiations went on for an extended period of time. In fact, they went on for so long that I was unable to hear the case that day. Ultimately, at the end of the day the parties were unable to reach a resolution. After brief oral arguments in court, I granted the ADA's motion to continue the case.

Due to the emotionally charged nature of this case, I knew I needed to hear the testimony, and see the evidence as soon as possible. The earliest available time on my docket was a full day on June 15th and a half day June 16, 2005. I set the case for those days and came off the bench frustrated that the parties were not ready for trial.

I had a conversation with every attorney involved in this case prior to the June 15th hearing. I informed each of them that if a settlement agreement was to be reached, it must be done before the time of the trial. I did not want a situation just like the June 6th hearing, where a hallway full of witnesses waited on attorneys to negotiate. When the negotiations failed, I would be required to, once again, continue the case. During this conversation I had with each attorney, I advised them that we would start the trial at 9am sharp on June 15th and we would go late into the evening. I would then return early on the morning of the 16th and would try the case until 1pm. After that time, we would have to return in July if we did not finish the case.

I told the attorneys I was set to leave on vacation the evening of the 16th. However, there was more than sufficient time, either before my vacation, if all attorneys had a chance to call their witnesses, or when we returned in July if we were unable to complete the trial on 16th.

The parties continued negotiations, but ultimately decided to go to trial. On Wednesday, June 15, 2005, all parties, along with their attorneys reappeared in my courtroom to provide testimony and evidence regarding the care and custody of Kelsey Smith-Briggs.

From where I sat on the bench, Royce and Kathie Briggs were on the counsel table to my left, with Royce farthest against the wall. He wore a blue gray suit, remained expressionless, and oftentimes leaning against the wall with his shoulder.

Kathie always seemed to dress in plain clothing. On this day, she wore a beige dress and sat in the middle of Royce and their attorney. She appeared to be taking a lot of notes and passing them to her attorney, who sat by the aisle, while others were testifying. When it was her turn to testify, her demeanor would change with each attorney. For her attorney she was open, seemed forthcoming, but for every other attorney she was closed off, with her arms crossed in front of her.

On the counsel table to my right, the Assistant District Attorney sat alone. He was not the usual ADA to handle this case. An ADA from Pottawatomie County was assigned this case, because the usual ADA had a military obligation.

Raye Dawn and her attorney sat in the first two chairs in the jury box, which was to my far right. Some may have seen Raye Dawn as someone cold, callous, and without feelings, but it was clear to me that she came to fight for the return of her child.

The jury box had six seats in the front row and six in the back. Two seats down from them was Kelsey's attorney. On the last seat, at the end of the jury box, was the CASA worker. The seat directly behind her was her supervisor, who had been with her every step of the way during her investigations of this case.

Immediately in front of me, on my left, was my clerk/bailiff for juvenile cases, Bonnie. She is a very sweet lady in her late 40s, and is dedicated to her job. It was nice to have such a professional alongside me in such cases.

Gayla Smith, Raye Dawn's mother, waited in the hallway, along with the other witnesses. That day I remember she wore a black pantsuit, with perfect hair and flawless makeup.

The Meeker police officers, who had testified at the February hearing, also waited in the hallway. They each have testified in many other cases, and were extremely professional on the stand, and only answered the questions they were asked when it was their turn.

Michael Porter testified on behalf of Raye Dawn. He is a big guy, dark hair, at approximately 6'3" and 240 pounds. He seemed clean cut and articulate. As he sat on the witness stand, immediately to my right, I watched him closely as he spoke and answered questions. I was trying to read him, get a feel of what this man was about, and at the time, I believed what he was saying. However, looking back, I feel like I may have completely misread Michael Porter. He seemed to be an upstanding guy as he talked of having voluntarily taking parenting classes, without even being asked. He was raising his eight-year-old daughter, and saw his son, who had a different mom than his daughter, several days a week. He appeared to be a man that was committed to his own children as he spoke about the volumes of allegations of child abuse that had been raised by the paternal family.

Everyone, from the mother of one of his children, to his former mother-in-law had nothing to say about him that was negative.

When Porter was arrested for Kelsey's death, I lied in bed for the next several nights, wondering if he was a wolf in sheep's clothing. One of the greatest disappointments in this case is the fact that a jury will never hear evidence and determine who murdered Kelsey.

In the meantime, our task at hand was to determine where Kelsey should be placed. A former Lincoln County child welfare worker, who had recently transferred to Seminole County, concluded that Raye Dawn was the one responsible for the bruises on Kelsey's buttocks. Since Raye Dawn had custody of Kelsey at the time the bruising occurred, DHS automatically looked at her as the prime suspect. DHS had ruled out abuse on the clavicle break (collarbone) and bruising to the head that had occurred in January.

When Kelsey had the first leg fracture, the DHS wasn't concerned with the injury, because it was plausible. However, when a second opinion showed that the fractures occurred on two separate occasions, they became very involved with trying to determine the perpetrator. DHS was only able to narrow the timeline to show that the fractures occurred when Kelsey was in the care of Kathie Briggs from April 18th to April 21st, or with Raye Dawn Smith from April 21st to April 25th, during which time, multiple people had access to Kelsey. They narrowed down the time that it occurred, but not the person who did it.

While Mike Porter was fairly new to Kelsey's life, DHS did check into several character witnesses from the maternal sides of his children's families. All of his character witnesses stated he was caring and attentive to his children, and an outstanding father. In addition, Porter had no prior DHS referrals or contacts. Because of the information they received, DHS was unable to make a determination as an outcome of those investigations. Since he was around Kelsey during the timeframe her legs were broken, DHS could not rule him out as the perpetrator for the abuse.

Allegations of Porter hurting Kelsey came from Ashley Briggs. Ashley told DHS that her brother, a child, asked Kelsey who hurt her. According to the child, Kelsey said Mike had hurt her by throwing her or pushing her off the bed. These allegations were never confirmed by DHS.

At that point the Briggs became possible perpetrators of abuse on Kelsey, and Kelsey was removed from their home and taken into protective custody.

Kelsey's leg first became injured when Raye Dawn's sister-in-law, Miste Smith, had taken Kelsey to the zoo on April 14, 2005. Kelsey fell and was diagnosed that day with a sprain. Raye Dawn was instructed to keep her walking on it so that it would not become stiff.

When Raye Dawn brought Kelsey to Kathie later that same day with a doctor's note, Kathie called DHS. It was after 5pm, so she called the hotline to report the injury. She did not get a call back until the next morning.

The following day Raye Dawn picked Kelsey up at 9:15am on and took her to the DHS office in Chandler, and kept her until 5pm on the 18th. Raye Dawn would have normally gotten Kelsey on Wednesday and taken her back Thursday, but instead she got her on Thursday, April 21, 2005 for a long weekend.

When Raye Dawn picked Kelsey up, she asked Kathie why Kelsey was crawling. Kelsey was supposed to be walking on it, and Kathie told

Raye Dawn that earlier that week Kelsey had taken four steps in Wal-Mart, fell down, cried, and didn't want to walk anymore.

According to Kathie, Kelsey did not complain about her leg during that time. Kathie said Kelsey tried to stand a few times during the week next to furniture, but did not really try to walk. Kathie was not concerned about Kelsey not walking because she had a sprained ankle.

What bothered me most about this is the fact that Kathie did not take her to the doctor. When Kelsey could not walk, Kathie saw no need to get a second opinion. Ultimately, Kathie waited until Raye Dawn took Kelsey to the doctor and had casts put on Kelsey's legs to take her to the doctor. This really made no sense to me whatsoever because Kathie was constantly calling and sending emails to DHS with every little bump, bruise, or scratch she found on Kelsey. Why take Kelsey to the emergency room for a bruise and ignore the fact that she couldn't walk?

Raye Dawn picked Kelsey up on the 21st, but waited until the 25th to take her to the doctor because she thought that Kelsey's foot had become stiff since she had not walked at Kathie's. This troubled me as well. Why wait four days to take Kelsey to the doctor when she was not walking? During that time, Raye Dawn continued to make Kelsey walk, thinking she was doing what she was supposed to do. But when Kelsey's legs became hot and swollen and she would cry every time Raye Dawn had her stand up, she immediately took Kelsey to DHS, who advised Raye Dawn to take Kelsey to the doctor. She took her to Dr. Koons who referred her to Dr. Barrett. Her legs were cast and she was told that the right leg was consistent with what happened at the zoo and the left one may have been a newer injury. The doctor said it didn't seem like abuse, because it wasn't uncommon for kids to come in with two broken legs. She'd seen one like it just the week before that.

Kathie planned to go with Raye Dawn to get Kelsey's legs in casts, but Kathie said the appointment was moved forward two hours and she was not notified.

Dr. Koons then recommended a bone density testing, so Gayla and Raye Dawn both took Kelsey for her appointment.

Another thing that really concerned me was that Kathie had the casts removed from Kelsey's fractured legs at Children's hospital on May 2, 2005.

Kathie told Raye Dawn that she was taking Kelsey to OU for a genetics testing for the bone density. Raye Dawn couldn't go to the appointment with her, because her great-grandmother's funeral was the same day. Kathie disputes Raye Dawn's reason for not going to the doctor's appointment at OU Medical Center. According to Kathie, Raye Dawn was afraid they would suspect abuse and Kelsey would be taken into DHS custody. Kathie told Raye Dawn that she did not think anyone would suspect abuse, because she had taken her to a Shawnee doctor who said it was growth plates.

According to Kathie, Dr. Sullivan said it was abuse that caused the injuries to Kelsey's legs. However, Dr. Sullivan's conclusions came after Kathie informed him of the previous allegations with regards to Kelsey. He took off the casts, because he said they were too high on Kelsey's legs and she did not need them on for more than two weeks.

Kathie took Kelsey to the doctor for a bump on the nose, but when Kelsey could not walk, she did not take her to the doctor. Kathie waited until the child was already in casts. Then she had the casts removed, and Kelsey was, once again, unable to walk. Kathie claimed that she only took Kelsey to the doctor for the bump on the nose to make sure it wasn't broken, but what about her legs?

Kelsey was placed in protective custody by DHS and given to Gayla Smith while the case was pending. After Kelsey's casts were removed, Kelsey was in pain and refused to walk, so Gayla Smith took her to Dr. Bennett on May 6th and the casts were put back on. Although the OU Medical Center doctor stated that a twisting and pushing down motion would be required to cause the fractures to Kelsey's legs. Never were any physical signs

Raye Dawn and Kelsey

Lance Briggs

Raye Dawn and her father, Ray Smith, at Lance and Raye Dawn's wedding, at the house that Raye Dawn and Porter purchased, where Kelsey died

Raye Dawn and Lance's Wedding
From left to right: Belvia Winter, Lance, Raye Dawn, Ray Smith, Gayla Smith, Mildred Fowler, Elvis Fowler

CERTIFICATE OF LIVE BIRTH

STATE OF OKLAHOMA-DEPARTMENT OF HEALTH

02-047400

0211000002166- 1   STATE FILE NO. 135-

1. CHILD'S NAME (First, Middle, Last)	2. DATE OF BIRTH (Month, Day, Year)	3. TIME OF BIRTH
KELSEY SHELTON SMITH	December 28, 2002	10:00 PM

4. SEX	5. CITY, TOWN, OR LOCATION OF BIRTH	6. COUNTY OF BIRTH
Female	Oklahoma City	Oklahoma

7. PLACE OF BIRTH	8. FACILITY NAME (If not institution, give street and number)
Hospital	OU MEDICAL CENTER PRESBYTERIAN TOWER

9. I certify that the child was born alive at the place and time on the date stated. Signature	10. DATE SIGNED 12-29-02	11. ATTENDANT'S NAME AND TITLE (If other than certifier) (Type/Print) Name GOFF, DARREN Title M.D.

12. CERTIFIER'S NAME AND TITLE (Type/Print) Name CAMPBELL ANGELIA Title CERTIFIER	13. ATTENDANT'S MAILING ADDRESS
14. DATE RECEIVED BY LOCAL REGISTRAR JAN 0 7 2003	Street and Number or Rural Route 825 NE 10TH ST SUITE 3300 City or Town Oklahoma City State Oklahoma 73104-0000

15a. STATE REGISTRAR'S SIGNATURE	15b. DATE FILED BY STATE REGISTRAR (Month, Day, Year) JAN 0 7 2003

16a. MOTHER'S NAME (First, Middle, Last) RAYE DAWN SMITH		
16b. MAIDEN SURNAME SMITH	17. DATE OF BIRTH (Month, Day, Year) November 19, 1979	18. BIRTHPLACE (State or Foreign Country) Oklahoma
19a. RESIDENCE - STATE Oklahoma	19b. COUNTY Lincoln	19c. CITY, TOWN, OR LOCATION Meeker	19d. STREET AND NUMBER PO BOX 188
19e. INSIDE CITY LIMITS? Yes	20. MOTHER'S MAILING ADDRESS (If same as residence, enter Zip Code only) 74855-0000		

21. FATHER'S NAME (First, Middle, Last)	22. DATE OF BIRTH (Month, Day, Year)	23. BIRTHPLACE (State or Foreign Country)

24. Permission given to provide Social Security Administration with the necessary information to issue a Social Security Number. Yes Initals RS
25. I certify that the personal information provided on this certificate is correct to the best of my knowledge and belief. Signature of Parent Raye Smith

THIS LINE FOR USE OF STATE REGISTRAR	DATE CORRECTIONS MADE	ITEMS CORRECTED	AUTHORITY	CLERK

State Department of Health

State of Oklahoma

OKLAHOMA CITY, OKLAHOMA 73117

I hereby certify the foregoing to be a true and correct copy, original of which is on file in this office. In testimony whereof, I have hereunto subscribed my name and caused the official seal to be affixed, at Oklahoma City, Oklahoma, this date.

August 4, 2003

CERTIFIED COPY MUST BE VALIDATED IN THREE COLORS

STATE REGISTRAR

Kelsey's Birth Certificate

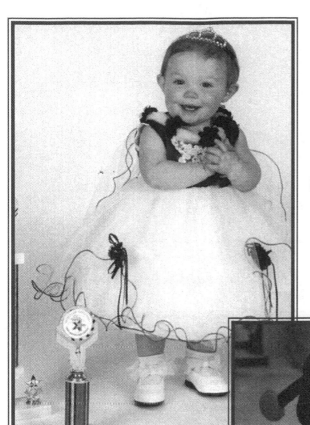

On January 28, 2004, one-year-old Kelsey Shelton Smith-Briggs was a contestant in the Most Beautiful Baby Pageant. She won Best Personality in her age group of 8-14 months, and qualified to go to state May 15, 2004, in Kansas.

Kelsey in her Halloween costume

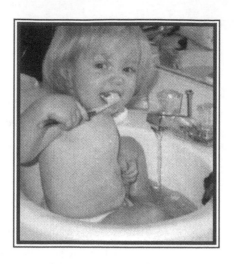

Kelsey was a climber!

Kelsey after a visitation with the Briggs in the winter of 2004

Kelsey in February, 2005

Raye Dawn and Mike Porter

The Smith — Porter home where Kelsey died

Porter and Kelsey at the Oklahoma City Zoo in June, 2005
Shortly after Kelsey's return to her mother, Raye Dawn

Kathie Briggs addresses the media

November 22, 2005, Approximately 30 people picketed outside the
Lincoln County Courthouse, asking for my resignation
Photo courtesy of *The Lincoln County News*

such as bruises or marks noticed on Kelsey's legs that would have been consistent with the required force to cause Kelsey's injuries.

> **Never were any physical signs such as bruises or marks noticed on Kelsey's legs that would have been consistent with the required force to cause Kelsey's injuries.**

Another concern I had was that Kathie had put Kelsey in gymnastics during that period, and with Kelsey going back and forth from home to home, there was no way to determine what had caused the injury or if, in fact, Kelsey had attended gymnastics, though Kathie denied that she took her.

Kathie's aunt alleged that Kelsey told her about her leg injury and that Mike had kicked her off the bed, her mommy yelled at him, and then they ate pizza and French fries.

She had accompanied Kathie to take Kelsey to see Dr. Sullivan about Kelsey's legs, after Raye Dawn had them put in casts. Allegedly, Kathie had mentioned to Dr. Sullivan about the abuse charges and the custody battle, because they were in shock that both of her legs were broken. It was after Kathie mentioned allegations of abuse and told the doctor that Kelsey had been with Raye Dawn when both legs were injured, which was not proven to be true, that the doctor said something about the injuries being from abuse.

The doctor told Kathie and her aunt that the injuries were intentional. Again, this was after the fact that Kathie had pointed out to the doctor that they suspected Kelsey was being abused.

According to Kathie's aunt, the casts had to come off Kelsey because she had sores under them that needed to heal, and her bones had started to heal.

Kathie's aunt visited Kathie's home during the time Kelsey's legs were injured. She thought Kelsey had a sprained ankle, so they just carried her around or she played in the floor and she didn't think anything about it.

She claimed she did not witness her not being able to walk without the casts after they were off, but she had heard that after the casts went back on, her legs were going inward a little bit and she was having trouble walking then.

At this point, DHS was questioning who had Kelsey when her legs were broken. The fact that Kathie called repeatedly to report abuse against Raye Dawn, yet did not take Kelsey to the doctor when she could not walk, made Kathie appear suspicious to DHS.

Kathie insisted throughout the case that she only called DHS one time. If she had actually called "one time" like she claimed, DHS would not have told her to ONLY call if it appeared that Kelsey had suffered from abuse. The simple fact that DHS had to tell her when to call and when not to call, tells me that she called them repeatedly. Kathie contradicted herself and claimed she had only made one or two reports since January.

In order to make her reports, Kathie kept record of Kelsey's bruises and injuries when she would return from a visit with Raye Dawn. She'd write the injury in the calendar and take a picture of it. She claimed that she didn't report them to DHS until Kelsey had a bruised nose from falling in Raye Dawn's apartment and Kathie took Kelsey to the emergency room on March 24, 2005.

When documenting Kelsey's alleged abuse, Kathie had three or four people look over Kelsey every time Kelsey came to her home from Raye Dawn's for signs of abuse, and they would examine Kelsey again before Kelsey left to go back to Raye Dawn's. She did not want anyone to accuse her of causing the injuries and she wanted to document anything she saw.

Kathie took pictures and documented every mark on the child when anything happened at Raye Dawn's. However, when Kelsey was hurt while at Kathie's, which happened on more than one occasion, no pictures were taken and nothing was documented.

Every time Kathie called DHS, she talked to one DHS worker. According to Kathie, this person told her at first to report every mark, and then she said only report them if she thought it was abuse. Allegedly, Kathie was scolded by the worker for not calling about the bump on her nose. According to Kathie, the doctor in the emergency room called about her sprained ankle.

From May 3rd to May 5th when Kelsey was taken into DHS custody, the Briggs family had supervised visitation. Their visits were also supervised when Kelsey was placed with Gayla while in DHS custody.

Kathie visited Kelsey for two hours every week at the DHS office. The CASA worker was provided notes from DHS workers who had supervised the visits between Kathie and Kelsey. The notes showed Kelsey bit, pinched, hid under blankets, tore up books, and sometimes screamed at Kathie when she would visit Kelsey at the DHS office. Kathie claimed that wasn't true and that Kelsey screamed because she had taken scissors away from her. Kathie also claimed Kelsey scratched her when a DHS worker tried to take her away from her for a doctor's visit.

She denied being bitten by Kelsey while being observed and claimed that Kelsey scratched her and acted cranky when she would get tired. Yet again, in Kelsey's obituary she stated among Kelsey's favorite things to do was biting. All of the documentation by DHS directly contradicts Kathie's claims regarding Kelsey's reactions to her during supervised visits. But DHS noted that Kelsey always ran to and loved on her mother, Raye Dawn, during her supervised visits, some on the same day as Kathie's visit. Yet, Kathie wanted to regain guardianship of Kelsey until Mike and Raye Dawn had classes or they figured out what happened to Kelsey. DHS did not see the Briggs home as an appropriate setting for Kelsey due to the questions about Kelsey's fractured legs and Kelsey's reaction to Kathie's visits.

In addition to Kathie's visits, Ashley and Royce Briggs shared in some of the supervised visitation with Kelsey, even though they were not specified visitation in the court order. Based on the DHS case worker, it was her recommendation that guardianship of Kelsey would never be returned to Kathie Briggs.

Kelsey continued to show physical signs of improvement while she was living with her maternal grandmother, Gayla Smith.

The DHS investigator also witnessed Kelsey losing her hair to the point that she had a bald spot the size of a baseball while living with Kathie Briggs. As soon as Kelsey was taken into DHS custody in May and then placed with her maternal grandmother, Gayla, she gained weight and her hair stopped falling out and eventually began to grow back. Kelsey continued to show physical signs of improvement while she was living with her maternal grandmother, Gayla Smith.

Another DHS investigator at the June hearing believed that Kelsey should not be returned to Kathie's home. DHS wanted to see Raye Dawn regain custody of Kelsey, because DHS works with the parents to keep the child with the parents whenever possible. DHS's stance was that Kelsey should not be returned to the Briggs' home, but left with Gayla until Kelsey was phased into Raye Dawn's home through CHBS A phase-in plan requires a six to eight week period, during which time the number of nights a child stays in the parent's home is increased until the child resides full-time with the parent. According to the testimony of this DHS worker, other than CHBS phasing Kelsey into the home, Raye Dawn had satisfied all requirements of her treatment plan to take custody of Kelsey once more.

If the Briggs were to regain guardianship of Kelsey, Gayla worried that because Lance had abused Raye Dawn during their relationship, Kelsey may suffer the same fate. In the fall of 2004, when Kathie began having visitation, Kelsey came back from Kathie's with bruises that both Gayla and Raye Dawn questioned could have been from abuse. Gayla, like Julie, had thought that some of the bruises looked like someone had grabbed Kelsey by the knees.

Gayla wanted to retain guardianship of Kelsey. However, she had no concerns about Raye Dawn's ability to care for Kelsey. She knew Raye

Dawn took care of Kelsey, because Kelsey would run to Raye Dawn and talk to her on their visits.

At the June hearing Gayla truly believed that Kelsey needed to go back home with her mom. On several occasions Kelsey would cry and scream that she wanted her mommy. During the spring, Raye Dawn was at DHS when Gayla called to tell her that Kathie had called her because Kelsey was crying for her mom. Raye Dawn immediately left DHS and went to Kathie's to take care of her daughter. *Why couldn't the parties have communicated like this throughout this entire ordeal?* In Gayla's opinion, Raye Dawn would never harm her daughter or allow anyone else to touch her, and she felt Kelsey belonged with her mom.

According to the opinion of DHS, any time that there was an injury to Kelsey, Raye Dawn would seek appropriate medical attention within an appropriate timeframe. DHS always found Raye Dawn to be completely cooperative throughout this entire process. DHS now was aware of the history of abuse that Raye Dawn suffered at the hands of Lance, and that Raye Dawn had no history of abuse or violence against anyone.

As for the bruises that occurred between January and April, at the time of this hearing, they were still being investigated. However, DHS was never concerned enough to stop Raye Dawn's visitation with her daughter. This was true, even though many of the bruises had occurred while in Raye Dawn's care. A DHS investigator confirmed that Kelsey was a rambunctious child, bruised easily, and that Kathie had made several allegations of abuse against Raye Dawn from January until April. DHS always found Raye Dawn's explanations for Kelsey's bruising to be plausible. The documented abuse spoken of on news reports is not in the nature that led DHS to confirm child abuse and ask for her visitation to stop. The only confirmed abuse was the bruising on Kelsey's buttocks in January, 2005, and her fractured legs in April, 2005. When each of these incidents occurred, both Kathie and Raye Dawn had been with Kelsey.

From January until the hearing in June, it was alleged that Kathie had followed Raye Dawn and made police reports against her for speeding and reckless driving. All of the allegations by Kathie were determined by DHS and the Meeker Police Department to be unfounded.

At this hearing, Raye Dawn stated she felt Kathie took Kelsey to the doctor for everything. She even allegedly had her allergy tested during her guardianship, even though Kelsey showed no signs of allergies. Raye Dawn felt Kelsey took medicine nonstop while at Kathie's home, which she believed was the reason that each time Kathie took Kelsey to DHS she was asleep.

DHS had their concerns and suspicions about Kathie, but there were no complaints about Raye Dawn from any of the DHS staff. Raye Dawn had done everything DHS requested and had completed every requirement of her treatment plan. Her plan had included parenting classes, a domestic violence program, a drug and alcohol assessment, and anger management. She had completed a 12-week parenting course and a domestic violence inventory. Based on the drug and alcohol assessment and the domestic violence inventory, it was determined that Raye Dawn had a low risk for lying, abusing alcohol, almost nonexistent for control, almost nonexistent for drugs, and a low risk for violence. It also showed that she had a medium risk for stress coping. Along with the domestic violence inventory, her counselor provided a letter that stated a follow-up group would not be necessary and that Raye Dawn had no need for a domestic violence course. Her anger management counselor had provided DHS with a letter indicating that additional domestic violence classes would not be necessary because of her low likelihood of violence.

A CHBS worker had been set up in Raye Dawn's home, and she went through an assessment for grief counseling for the loss of her father and great-grandmother and it was determined further counseling was not needed.

The only objection the DHS worker had to returning custody of Kelsey to Raye Dawn was the immediate return. She wanted CHBS to assist in phasing Kelsey back into Raye Dawn's home. The "phase-in" process is a six to eight week plan. Under a phase-in program, Kelsey would have spent two nights in Raye Dawn's home and five nights in Gayla's. The next week, she would have spent three nights in Raye Dawn's home, and four nights in Gayla's, and so on. There is no question that under either DHS's recommendation for phase-in, or the immediate placement of Kelsey back in her mother's home, that CHBS would have monitored Kelsey's progress. Based on what we know of Kelsey's progress from June 16th through July 31st, on August 1, 2005, Kelsey would have been in Raye Dawn's home full-time in either scenario.

In addition, DHS was not concerned with Kelsey being in the home with Michael Porter. DHS had observed Kelsey and Porter during the supervised visits in May and found Kelsey and Porter's relationship to be appropriate. Since Kathie had disobeyed the court order by knowingly allowing Michael Porter to be around Kelsey, DHS found it difficult to agree with her regarding Michael Porter being the perpetrator. Kathie, herself, saw nothing wrong with violating the court order in allowing Porter around Kelsey during late March and into April, 2005.

The only allegation that was substantiated by any report involving Porter was by Ashley Briggs. Ashley had filed a protective order against Porter in the spring alleging he was stalking her in Shawnee. After a hearing, a judge determined Ashley had failed to provide sufficient evidence to grant a protective order and her case was dismissed. According to Kathie, Porter had threatened her on April, 29th at about 3:15pm. She had received a letter saying Mike was going to sue for slander.

During this hearing, Porter made statements that he thought Raye Dawn was a good parent and he would like it if Kelsey came to live with them. He even voluntarily enrolled in parenting classes and was about to complete a class. According to him, he had no problems with anger management and had not seen a problem with Raye Dawn.

In regards to Lance, DHS had been told by Kathie that he was unreachable, or in Iraq each time they wanted to contact him about the investigation. They had not been able to reach him or confirm his army status and Kathie Briggs was uncooperative. In fact, nobody with DHS had heard from Lance since May, and he had not contacted them to find out what was going on with his daughter.

To everyone's surprise, the only times the DHS worker had talked to Lance Briggs was by telephone during the months that the struggle over Kelsey was at its peak in March and April, 2005, she had never met with him in person. Every time the DHS worker spoke to Lance from March to April, it was on his cell phone, and instead of being in Iraq, as his mother had said, Lance told the worker he was driving around Shawnee, Oklahoma.

> Every time the DHS worker spoke to Lance from March to April, it was on his cell phone, and instead of being in Iraq, as his mother had said, Lance told the worker he was driving around Shawnee, Oklahoma.

During the course of her investigation, the CASA worker looked at everyone, including Raye Dawn, as a possible perpetrator. The CASA worker found no evidence that Raye Dawn was the perpetrator. She attempted to contact Lance, even though he was in Lincoln County in April, and she could not find him, because DHS had no record of his address or phone number. DHS had tried to contact him and it was like he disappeared. There was no military information on him whatsoever or any information on where he was stationed. She even asked for a subpoena to get records to try to find him, but without his family's cooperation, he was impossible to find. During the months of January, February, March, and April DHS confirmed that he was in the state of Oklahoma the few times they heard from him.

According to Lance's family members, Lance had been stationed in New York while waiting to go to Iraq. He had been seen several times since January, and his family had a birthday party for him in April.

Kathie claimed Lance had been in Oklahoma from April 4th to April 11th, and was in Iraq at the time of the hearing. She had just gotten his address two weeks before, and claimed that she had never been asked for his address by DHS. This is contrary to DHS reports.

According to Kathie, a DHS worker had asked for Lance's phone number on the day he landed in Iraq and she didn't have a number for him at that time. Later, she admitted she always knew where he was, but DHS didn't ask for the information at the time that she had it. This is another contradiction by Kathie, based on testimony and DHS documents.

It is well-documented of the continual efforts by DHS to contact Lance. As a judge, I knew the military would allow Lance to come home for the sake of his daughter, if only we could get in contact with him.

Based on information provided by Kathie, Lance's delay in going to Iraq was because he was injured in training. He had been stationed in Missouri at Fort Leonard Wood until the second week in February, and then went to Fort Dix, New Jersey, and then to Fort Benning, Georgia, until he departed and landed in Kuwait on May 3rd.

According to Kathie, Lance came home in April and Kathie allowed him to see Kelsey, instead of Raye Dawn. Kathie understood that Lance would have priority in seeing his daughter. She intended to make up the time to Raye Dawn at a later date.

According to Kathie, Lance had been in New Jersey for about two months before he flew home April 11th. He then went back to New Jersey for a few days, before going to Georgia for less than a week prior to being shipped overseas. Kathie's account of his whereabouts was totally contrary to DHS. DHS could not understand why Kathie would not provide information on how to reach Lance to ensure that he would be involved in the process. Instead, it appeared to DHS that Kathie was hiding something.

It was ironic that Lance was only gone from home for the hearings. He had been in Missouri in January and had come back in February. He left the day of the guardianship hearing to go back to Missouri to take care of his medical leave, yet he returned to Oklahoma that night. He left again on February 6th. Kathie did not know if he asked his commanding officer to be present for the guardianship hearing, because she said he was ordered back to Missouri. Lance did not appear at ANY hearing that involved guardianship of Kelsey.

One of the witnesses who testified at the June hearing was a relative of both the Smith and Briggs families. She had been married to Gayla's brother, had known Gayla for almost 40 years, and had some harsh things to say about Raye Dawn. At the time of the hearing, her son was also married to Kathie's daughter.

Allegedly, Gayla had told her that Raye Dawn would fly into rages where she would have a bad attitude. She would yell and was hard to get along with. The last incident that she knew of this type of behavior had occurred a year earlier.

Allegedly, Gayla had also told her that Raye Dawn would "kill" Ashley Briggs if she got custody of Kelsey. She claimed that Gayla had to blow into Raye Dawn's breathalyzer machine a year earlier to start her car for her in the morning. Later, she admitted that the reason for Gayla's assistance was because Raye Dawn had brushed her teeth and used mouth wash. She also claimed to know that Mike Porter had watched Kelsey while Raye Dawn went to one of her classes for the case.

Although she and Gayla were friends, she had not talked to her since February, 2005. Allegedly, this same person had emailed Gayla, saying that the Briggs family was "psycho" and she hoped that Raye Dawn got custody of Kelsey. In court she denied using the word "psycho." However, it is easy to infer that she believed that Kelsey should be with Raye Dawn. She did not think Raye Dawn had hurt Kelsey, but she thought Raye Dawn knew who did. She thought Raye Dawn should get Kelsey, because she was her mother, and that even Kathie thought Raye Dawn should have Kelsey.

I remember sitting on the bench wondering if Kathie thought Raye Dawn should have Kelsey, then why were we in court? This person thought Kathie was protecting her grandchild. According to this witness, Kathie wanted Raye Dawn to straighten up and then get Kelsey because she didn't want to raise a child. She claimed to be friends with Kathie Briggs, but better friends with Gayla Smith. She thought Kathie was a good person, and she had heard both Gayla and Raye Dawn say that they knew Kathie would be good to Kelsey.

The most scrutinized testimony from the hearing was from the CASA worker, who was employed with Project Heart, the Lincoln County outreach program. She had interviewed Assistant Chief of Meeker P.D., Matt Byers; Chief Connor of the Meeker P.D.; Gayla Smith; DHS; a close friend who was like a sister, who worked with Raye Dawn for several years at Lewis Manufacturing; and Julie, the owner of Kelsey's daycare. In addition, the CASA worker reviewed all of the court and DHS files. She also unsuccessfully attempted to contact Lance before making her recommendation.

The CASA worker's friend said that Raye Dawn was a good mother and was always trying to keep Kelsey from getting into things when she brought her to the plant. Kelsey was described as being hyper and always into everything.

During cross-examination, it was revealed that the CASA worker had only completed her training six weeks earlier. In my opinion, the criticism of this CASA worker is unfair. Her supervisor was with her every step of the way and based on the mountains of reports she reviewed, her attempts to contact Lance, as well as her personal interviews, the media has improperly portrayed this worker.

The bottom line for her was the fact that everything she had seen in her investigation and everything she had heard in court did not alter the fact that she could not find any evidence that justified denying Raye Dawn custody of Kelsey. Later, the CASA worker admitted to being influenced, because of the fact that until the hearing, the DHS workers had planned on recommending Kelsey go back with her mother.

The agencies charged with investigating this case were unable to make a determination based on information Lance provided. Those who tried to gain contact information in order to interview Lance were shut down by Kathie Briggs. Kathie informed them that he was in the war fighting for our country, and she didn't want to put him in a dangerous situation.

We took a recess at around 3pm. I was sitting in my office drinking a Diet Dr. Pepper, trying to make heads or tails of all the conflicting testimony, when Sheila Kirk walked in. She asked what I was doing, and I told her of the case. She informed me that she knew both parties, and in her words: the Smiths were a nice and good family, and Kathie Briggs was "white trash." At that point, I held up my hand as to say "stop." Looking back, maybe she was trying to influence me somehow on behalf of the Smiths.

I've always thought it was interesting that during the election of 2006 she would describe Kathie as a saint and a great lady. Sheila and Kathie were inseparable. Later in the book, I'll cover all the allegations made by Sheila Kirk and Kathie Briggs during the election. If it is true that politics makes strange bedfellows, what occurred in this case, and during the 2006 campaign, is living proof.

At the end of the first day of the custody hearing, we had been through ten hours of testimony and everyone was exhausted. We adjourned for the night and were set to begin on the 16th at 7am. I let every attorney call every witness they wanted to call. There wasn't a single witness who was precluded from testifying. Time was never an issue.

That night was a sleepless night for me. When I was in the midst of a case, I paced the floor and often "tried to sleep" on the couch. This was definitely one of those nights. I struggled with this case and the decision that I would make the following day.

Early the following morning of the 16th, I went into the vault in the court clerk's office, where the attorneys gather to drink coffee and discuss cases, to get a cup of coffee. No one had arrived except for Bonnie, my bailiff. She walked over to the doorway separating the court clerk's office from the vault, gave me a puzzled look and asked, "How are you going to make heads or tails out of this one, Judge?" I answered, "I guess that's why I make the big bucks, to make decisions on cases like this." Those words have drummed through my mind since October 11, 2005. Although I was joking, I would have given everything up to just have Kelsey back for her families.

It seemed a nearly impossible decision to make with all the convoluted facts that I'd been given. The facts were so mixed up and contradictory intertwined. On the morning of the 16th, the only people who showed up to watch the tapes of both doctor's depositions was Kelsey's attorney, the CASA worker, and her supervisor. On the previous day, I had informed everyone in the courtroom that I would start the viewing of the depositions at 7:20am the following morning.

It was still unclear to me who was abusing Kelsey. According to DHS, the evidence pointed to either family. Raye Dawn had completed what was required of her by DHS, and except for a six week "phase in" program, DHS had no valid reason to keep Kelsey from her mother.

After reviewing a deposition by Dr. Barrett and watching a video deposition of Dr. Sullivan, I ultimately ruled that the guardianship order be dissolved and the custody of Kelsey Smith-Briggs would be turned back over to her mother, Raye Dawn Smith; Ashley Briggs would continue with regular visitation.

Afterthought

What remains puzzling to me to this very day is the fact that the photographs and home movies shown on television, in newspapers, and other sources of Kelsey's bruises and broken legs were never presented to me in court. *None of those pictures or videos were presented as evidence.* The first time I saw them was on the news. If I'm going to be judged by these photographs, I should have been allowed to see them before the decision was made to return Kelsey to her mother.

I made the decision based on what was provided to me through testimony of 13 witnesses and evidence presented in the courtroom.

After I returned Kelsey, there were three critical incident reports done by a CHBS worker. These reports are over the worker's concerns about something that was occurring in the home. They sent the information to DHS for further investigation. I found out after Kelsey's death that these reports were in existence, but for some reason they were never presented to me.

Prior to the June hearing, the DHS workers even started to question what was going on because of several key factors: 1) Kelsey's reaction to Kathie Briggs during supervised visits, 2) Kathie's constant accusations against Raye Dawn, 3) Kathie's failure to comply with a court order, and 4) Kathie's refusal to cooperate in helping DHS contact Lance Briggs.

Kathie has released direct quotes from the transcripts of this hearing. In fact, Kathie Briggs and Sheila Kirk, both, quoted from the transcript during the election of 2006. One quote that Kathie and Sheila used against me in the campaign was as follows: "I know the local people don't, but if DHS disagrees with me, they can come down here and argue with me." To understand this statement, we must first examine the law. When the legislature amended the statutes following the Ryan Luke case, they provided that a child's attorney, District Attorney, or the Department of Human Services shall each have the absolute right to stop any judge from returning a child to a parent.

I knew this case had been staffed by DHS above the county level. I informed everyone in the courtroom that if they disagreed with me to please stop me by appealing my decision under the Ryan Luke law. All they had to do was orally announce their intention to appeal my decision, and Kelsey would have stayed with her maternal grandmother, Gayla Smith. Kathie Briggs also had the absolute right to appeal my decision because I dissolved her guardianship. However, no one objected to or appealed my ruling when I returned Kelsey to Raye Dawn. Yet, I have been held responsible, because I did not have a crystal ball.

This wasn't a case that fell through the cracks. Every attorney in that courtroom was aware of their right to appeal. At the time, no one saw a problem with my decision.

CHAPTER ELEVEN

DHS, CHBS and CASA Keeps an Eye on Kelsey and Her Family

After Kelsey returned to her mother, Raye Dawn, DHS kept a close eye on Kelsey, and along with other agencies, visited her on a regular basis monitoring for signs of abuse. Between June 16, 2005 and October 11, 2005 someone from one of the various agencies charged with overseeing Kelsey's welfare visited Kelsey in her home on 33 separate occasions. At the request of Raye Dawn, someone from one of these agencies went with Kelsey and Raye Dawn to almost every one of Kelsey's doctor visits. Apparently, during the course of these contacts, nothing was seen to warrant removing Kelsey from the home.

In August, Raye Dawn reported to DHS workers that Kelsey had begun to have night terrors and was going through a stage of self-mutilation. She was biting herself, picking at scabs, and would wake up in the middle of the night with what was ultimately diagnosed as seizures.

On August 16, 2005, a representative of DHS went along with Raye Dawn to take Kelsey to see Dr. Koons regarding Kelsey's mental and emotional health. At that appointment, it was discussed that Kelsey had swelling in her nostril, had been injuring herself, had lost weight as a result of losing her appetite, was vomiting, having night terrors, and was afraid to be away from Raye Dawn.

On August 18, 2005, a DHS worker visited Kelsey in her home and noticed a bruise on Kelsey's left cheek. The family explained that Kelsey pulled a ceramic lamp down on herself, resulting in the bruise. This incident was never reported to me, and I did not learn of it until after Kelsey's death.

On August 19, 2005, at 10:23 p.m. Michael Porter, Raye Dawn, and Kelsey were struck by a drunk driver. The Porters were driving through an intersection in Shawnee, Oklahoma when a drunk driver made a left hand turn into them, their vehicle. The drunk driver left the scene of the accident.

Kelsey had been riding in a toddler seat and sustained a reddened area around her left eye and bruising to her forehead, the bridge of her nose, and her abdomen. She also complained of pain in her abdomen and her elbow. (Pictures of Kelsey have been shown on TV and on various websites to rally against abuse. The photograph of her in a swing with bruises to her face was taken shortly after the automobile accident.)

Raye Dawn and Porter took Kelsey to the emergency room the night of the accident at approximately 12:30am. They waited to be seen by a physician until 2:45am. During this time, Kelsey was seen running around the emergency room, eating Doritos, and acting like a normal toddler. Raye Dawn reported the accident to DHS the following day and told them that the triage nurse didn't suspect internal injuries because Kelsey was so rambunctious. The family ultimately left the emergency room without having Kelsey seen.

Kelsey's appetite diminished even more after the accident and she refused to eat. On August 25th, Raye Dawn was accompanied by the CHBS worker to Dr. Koons' office. The doctor noted:

1. Bruise to her left hip.
2. Bruise on her left mandible.
3. Bruise on her left cheek.
4. Not as playful since she had been told she'd have to visit her step-mother for visitation.

5. Doctor notes revealed that most of the bruises were consistent with the accident, though excessive. She noted that something else may be going on to cause the other problems.

6. Kelsey had also been having seizures, which they had previously referred to as night terrors.

After Kelsey's visit with Ashley on August 29, 2005, a DHS abuse report was called in by Ashley stating that Kelsey was acting timid, had lost weight, and her eye was red. This report was "screened out" due to the fact that Kelsey's doctor had documented the injuries from the auto accident in her August 25th report.

On August 30th, Raye Dawn voluntarily took Kelsey to the Lincoln County DHS office and filled out an application for counseling to find out why Kelsey was showing signs of self-injurious behavior. At this point, the Oklahoma Commission on Children and Youth was monitoring this case, and assisted in getting Kelsey into play therapy.

Raye Dawn reported to the DHS worker, on that visit, that she was pregnant with Michael Porter's child.

In September, 2005, at the request of DHS, the District Attorney's office filed a motion with a doctor's note attached seeking to immediately stop all visitation with the paternal side of the family. Kelsey was having seizures, and her environment needed to be controlled in order to help determine what was triggering the seizures.

On September 7, 2005, DHS received an email from Ashley Briggs stating that she was divorcing Lance.

On September 8th, a hearing was held to stop the paternal family's visitation. At this hearing, it was indicated that the DA and DHS thought

Kathie was the perpetrator of Kelsey's leg injuries. DHS believed that Kathie had been trying to sabotage the reunification of Kelsey and Raye Dawn as far back as March and April of 2005. (Sabotage is a term used when a grandparent, aunt, uncle, foster parent, or anyone, attempts to make the natural parent look bad so that the parent cannot regain custody of their child in a deprived case.)

At this hearing, it was reported that things were going well with Kelsey in Raye Dawn's home. It was at this time that all parties present agreed that the decision to return Kelsey in June was the right decision. In fact, an oral motion was made by the Assistant District Attorney (ADA) and Kelsey's attorney to dismiss the entire case against Raye Dawn and to leave visitation decisions solely to Raye Dawn's discretion.

The ADA and the child's attorney followed me into my chambers, and we reviewed the Ryan Luke Law, put in place following the Ryan Luke case. Under that law, a case cannot be dismissed until six months of DHS supervision has taken place after the child has returned to the natural parent. In other words, the case cannot be dismissed for six months until it's determined that the child is going to be well-taken care of in his or her home. In addition, they reviewed the civil visitation case. If their goal was to let Raye Dawn control the visits with Kathie Briggs, Raye Dawn would be in violation of the visitation court order once the deprived case was dismissed.

All parties returned to the courtroom. The State's motion to dismiss the case was withdrawn. However, visitation with the paternal side of the family was temporarily stopped so that Kelsey could be monitored. No one from the paternal family was there to object or provide any argument for their visitation to continue. The paternal family had made abuse referrals to DHS consistently since January, 2005, yet they did not appear in court to fight for their visitation. I assumed the paternal family was no longer concerned about Kelsey's welfare since no one appeared on the day of the hearing.

Lance Briggs' Military Career in Iraq Unverified

The sacrifices that our military service men and women make for our country are tremendous and should never be minimized. Yet, at the same time, to falsely portray someone as a war hero shows blatant disrespect to those serving in our military. Lance Briggs has been portrayed as walking off the airplane in Georgia to learn of the death of his daughter. I mean no disrespect, but if we're going to look at the full picture of this case in this book, I must outline what's been learned regarding Mr. Briggs' military career.

As you will recall, in the fall of 2004, Kathie Briggs petitioned the court to be allowed to exercise Lance's visitation with Kelsey if and when Lance was away on active military duty. Kathie was granted her request. Julie, the owner of the daycare center where Kelsey stayed, began seeing and documenting bruises on Kelsey from the time Kathie's visitation began.

It was at the February, 2005, hearing that I began to question Lance's military obligation. I was told Lance was in Meeker until the morning of the guardianship hearing, and then left to return to Fort Leonard Wood, Missouri. However, he returned to Oklahoma that same night. In all of my judicial dealings with the military, any time a service member's child is being abused, the Red Cross can typically arrange for emergency leave to allow a soldier to attend to his family situation. I was never presented with a viable explanation for Lance's absence during this hearing.

What continued to raise red flags was how Lance was in Oklahoma randomly throughout March and April, including returning for his birthday. It was as if he could control his military obligation to be at home whenever he pleased, but why did he always miss Kelsey's court hearings? During Kathie's DHS supervised visits in May, 2005, it was odd to me that Lance called during many of her two hour visits, yet when Kathie was continually asked by DHS for Lance's contact information, she always had an excuse as to why she could not provide the information requested. *How is it that Lance always knew when to call, yet Kathie did not know how to reach him?*

Because of the lack of cooperation from Lance's family, at that point, DHS became doubtful that Lance was actually stationed in Iraq. Not only did DHS hit a stone wall where the Briggs family was concerned, but they also received no response from repeated attempts to contact Lance through the military.

> How is it that Lance always knew when to call, yet Kathie did not know how to reach him?

It was the CASA worker who learned of Lance's location. The CASA worker had gone to pay her insurance bill in Prague, Oklahoma, where Lance's sister worked. It was discovered that Lance had been in Fort Benning, Georgia, at a military hospital for observation. Lance's family expressed how upset they were at the amount of medication Lance was taking, because it was having a negative impact on him.

Finally, on September 23, 2005, Lance contacted DHS. He informed DHS that he was injured while driving a truck in Iraq. He stated his orders were sitting on someone's desk, and he should be home in the next two weeks. *Why was the public told Lance was injured in Iraq, but his sister let down her guard and informed the CASA worker of his actual whereabouts?*

Lance called DHS again on October 6, 2005, and apologized for having lied about what happened to him and his location. He admitted that he had been in Fort Benning, Georgia since at least September, 2005, and not in Iraq.

The next call DHS would receive from Lance was shortly after Kelsey's death. Lance asked the DHS worker how that worker would feel if he broke into the worker's house and killed a member of his family or his children. Lance went on to say it was not a threat, but a promise, and that worker needed to advise me that my children and family would pay as well. Because of this and other threats by Lance, the office of Inspector General guarded the Lincoln County DHS office for months, and I was required to hide my children and have 24-hour protection by the sheriff's office.

Afterthought

While I greatly appreciate Lance's service to our country, his military service is but another mystery in this case. I hope someday Mr. Briggs will release his military records and we will learn what happened to him during this period and why he was required to discharge from the service on August 1, 2006.

Why would Lance's family fail to be forthcoming regarding his military service during Kelsey's alleged abuse charges? How is it that a father who claimed to be deeply concerned for his daughter, fail to attend any hearings regarding her welfare, when he admitted to being in the area?

A Deadly Game of Tug of War

CHAPTER TWELVE

October, 2005
The Final Days

DHS, CASA, or CHBS had contact with Kelsey by phone, visit, home visit, or by going along with Raye Dawn to a doctor's appointment approximately 52 times from June 16th to October 11th. In 118 days there were approximately 52 documented occasions where someone was either talking to or checking on Kelsey. When you realize how much contact was made in this case and the manner in which the officials were watching this case, what happened next just does not make sense.

On October 7, 2005, a DHS worker visited the Porter home. Raye Dawn informed her that Kelsey seemed to be improving.

On October 11, 2005, from noon to 1:30 p.m. the CHBS case manager was in the Porter home. She made a note that Kelsey had a small purple bruise and a bandage on her finger. She enjoyed watching Kelsey play that day. As she was leaving, the worker saw a turtle next to her car. Raye Dawn called Kelsey out to see the turtle. Raye Dawn and Kelsey began playing with the turtle, as the CHBS worker said, "See you next week Sugar Booger." The CHBS worker drove off as Kelsey waved goodbye, standing next to her newfound turtle friend.

Raye Dawn and Kelsey returned to the house from the driveway and Raye Dawn grabbed Kelsey a box of raisins. The two went to Raye Dawn's bed where Kelsey played with her box of raisins as she dozed off for her afternoon nap. Raye Dawn got out of bed and got ready to drive to Shawnee to pick up Michael Porter's daughter from school.

Porter returned home from work to wait for a friend who was coming by to pick up a set of tires. As Raye Dawn left to pick up Porter's daughter, she showed him the turtle Kelsey had been playing with and then drove away.

When Raye Dawn returned home 30 to 40 minutes later, an ambulance was sitting in the driveway, lights flashing. Raye Dawn pushed her way into the ambulance and told the EMTs that Kelsey had been suffering from seizures. She rode in the ambulance to the Prague Hospital alongside her daughter, crying, and saying, "Come on Kelsey, Come on Kelsey."

At 4:45pm on October 11, 2005, Kelsey Smith-Briggs was pronounced dead at the Prague Hospital in Prague, Oklahoma.

Afterthought

Kelsey was a bubbly ray of sunshine. It is impossible to comprehend how anyone could harm a child, much less have something happen when so many were watching so closely. The lesson from Kelsey's death is not only a cry to stop child abuse, but a reminder to cherish the little ones in our lives, and a warning to those embroiled in custody battles to take the focus off themselves and put it where it belongs, on the innocent children who did not ask to be a pawn in someone's game.

CHAPTER THIRTEEN

Death Threats

I forced myself to go to work the day after Kelsey died. The last thing I wanted to do was deal with people's problems, but I felt obligated to do my job. The sheriff called me into his office that afternoon and informed me they had talked to Lance Briggs the night before to tell him of the death of Kelsey, and that he was in Fort Benning, Georgia. The sheriff indicated that Lance was in some type of a treatment center, and that Lance had made threats against my family and me.

At that point, the sheriff was concerned because he told me he had spoken to people who were concerned with Lance's mental instability. The death threats that were made had come directly from Lance. It was a threat against my children, as well as the supervisor for DHS and his family.

"I don't put much stock in that. He's just upset and talking irrationally." I responded. But he told me there was little or no doubt that he had a fear for my children's lives and he wanted to put a deputy outside of my house and for me to get my children placed away from me.

Death threats on an attorney or a judge occur on occasion. Typically, they are not taken seriously. However, what convinced me to take action as a result of this threat was when I received a call from an OSBI agent, who confirmed what the sheriff had told me. DHS received the same information regarding Lance's threat. In order to protect their staff, the office of the Inspector General was dispatched to the Lincoln County DHS office. I knew of Lance's past history of domestic abuse, and with his current mental state, I chose to not take a chance with my family.

At the urging of all three law enforcement agencies, I decided to place my children with their grandparents, and to allow the sheriff to guard my house. Dana stayed home with me, and we were instructed not to have any personal contact with the children whatsoever. We could not go to the schools, their activities, or see them for four days. We talked to them on the telephone at night, but that was the extent of our contact. We treated this as a "holiday" for them, and their grandparents played along. At the time, I did not realize how much more protection we would need to provide for our children.

Dana and I were guarded at all times by the sheriff or one of his deputies.

These events made Dana extremely nervous and upset. We had to hide out our children. We discussed the ramifications of not taking appropriate precautions. This wasn't the first time there was I had experienced threats of this nature as a judge, though it was the first time that Dana had been aware of the possibility of something happening to our family because of my job.

During that time, Dana spent time crying, missing our girls, and wondering how long this would continue.

George Johnson, the spokesman for DHS, was experiencing similar problems during this time. I did not know George Johnson personally, but I came to know his face as he was at the forefront of defending DHS in the media.

One day the Oklahoma Commission on Children and Youth (OCCY) requested that I come to their office. They asked me to go over information that was never told to me during any of the hearings on Kelsey. After having met with OCCY, I left and went to eat lunch. I was by myself in the restaurant and extremely confused, because all of a sudden I was learning information that had never been revealed. I was playing a "what if" game and wondering if only I had known the withheld information, would Kelsey still be alive.

I was sitting there eating, and across the restaurant I recognized George Johnson. I got up and walked over and asked, "Are you George Johnson?" He never looked up. He just kept eating and he answered, "Not today." I said, "Today, I'm Judge Craig Key." At that point George stood up, smiled, and shook my hand. We were both apologetic for what was going on, and the fact that there was so much misinformation being provided to the public.

I expressed to him how I felt the criticism he personally was experiencing was wrong. I also let him know how sorry I was for it. We had a brief discussion, shook hands, and expressed our gratitude to each other for the honorable way we had dealt with this issue with the media, over which we had no control. It was a pretty touching moment for me. I think it brought a tear, literally, to both of our eyes. I let him know I was praying for him, and he reciprocated the gesture.

Afterthought

George Johnson is still with DHS to this day. He's their spokesman, and has been with DHS for a long time. He's a good man. What people often fail to realize, when it comes to George, is that his job is to defend DHS.

To this day, I look for a plaque for him that says, "Don't Shoot the Messenger."

A Deadly Game of Tug of War

CHAPTER FOURTEEN

Two Obituaries and Two Funerals

Is in the joyous news of her birth, Kelsey's death was announced separately, by both families. There were two obituaries and two separate funerals, just as there had been two birth announcements for Kelsey.

It started from birth, and ended with death. Both obituaries were in the local newspaper on the same day, Saturday, October 15, 2005. It's just unbelievably ironic the way these families fought to the bitter end, and beyond.

The Smith family obituary:

Kelsey Shelton Smith

"Kelsey Shelton Smith departed this life on Oct. 11, 2005, at the tender age of two years, nine months, and two weeks, at her home in Meeker.

Kelsey was born Dec. 28, 2002, in Oklahoma City to Raye Dawn (Smith) Porter and Lance Robinson (Briggs).

Kelsey loved to dance, and do the cha-cha with her mommy. She loved playing with her brother and sister and loved riding roller coasters with mommy. She would do anything as long as her mommy did it with her. She was always waiting on Grandma Gayla, because they would do everything together that people could possible think of. Kelsey always looked forward to her cousins… coming to stay the weekend with her. Kelsey's favorite movies were "Shrek,"

"Stuart Little 2," and "Monster's Inc." Most of all, she loved to lie down and sleep with her mommy, whether it be just a little nap or all night long.

She was preceded in death by her papa, Ray Shelton Smith... Survivors include her mommy, Raye Dawn (Smith) Porter; step-father, Mike Porter...Service will be 2p.m. Saturday at the Assembly of God Church in Meeker... Burial will follow at New Hope Cemetery in Meeker under the direction of Parks Brothers Funeral Service in Meeker.

Viewing and visitation will be 9a.m. to 12p.m. Saturday at Parks Brothers Funeral Chapel in Prague..."

The Briggs family obituary:

Kelsey Briggs

A funeral service for the Briggs family and friends of Kelsey Briggs, 2 1/2, will be 10a.m. today at Parks Brothers Funeral Home, Prague.

Kelsey was born Dec. 28, 2002, to Lance Briggs and Raye Dawn Porter.

She died Oct. 11, 2005 at Prague Hospital.

She loved swinging and gymnastics and riding her John Deere tractor. She also loved to bite.

Kelsey is survived by her father, SPC Lance Briggs of Fort Benning, GA; paternal grandparents, Royce and Kathie Briggs of Meeker... and numerous other family members and friends.

> The Briggs obituary stated among Kelsey's favorite things to do was "she also loved to bite."

The Briggs refused to attend the same funeral as the Smiths, and the Smiths refused to attend the Briggs funeral. Therefore two separate funerals were planned. However, the Smith family funeral was cut short when a bomb threat was made during the services. The entire gathering of family and friends were forced to leave the church and wait until the coast was clear before they could resume the services.

Just as the Briggs had recognized only their own family in Kelsey's birth announcement, the Briggs family, and friends of Kelsey Briggs were the only ones invited in the obituary provided by the Briggs on Kelsey's behalf.

Afterthought

What appeared to be a restricted invitation to celebrate Kelsey's life by the Briggs, is but one more clue of the brutal battle between the families that continues to this day.

A Deadly Game of Tug of War

CHAPTER FIFTEEN

Media Storm

After all that had occurred, the media put such a spin on the nightly news and in the morning papers of the events leading up to Kelsey's death. It was like a slow boil that all of a sudden just grew out of the pot, went into the flames of the fire, and just erupted.

Out of 52 child deaths that occurred in the State of Oklahoma in the year 2005, this one garnered 100% more attention than any of the others prior or since. Think about that, one death per week, but what laws were passed to recognize the children in the other 51 deaths? *Why haven't members of the legislature had their pictures taken for laws passed to protect these other children?*

Shortly following Kelsey's death, pictures and video of Kelsey with bruises or casts were shown continuously on the nightly news. Dana and I Tivo'd two of the 10pm newscasts and watched the other, so that we caught every single report that was coming out on the three major networks. Dana would ask me, "My God, did she look like that?" I shook my head "NO" and stared at the television with shock and surprise. I just kept asking Dana, "Why didn't they show me these pictures at the hearings?"

There is not one picture or video that they showed on television during that time that was ever presented to me in court. If they want me to make decisions based on what they show in the media, they should at least show it in court.

The media kept showing photos and vides, at this point, and was going nuts. It was probably mid November and I was hounded daily to talk, though I refused. If a reporter knocked on my office door, We would go into my office and I would inform him or her that I was not granting any interviews. I simply said, "Thank you very much for the opportunity to talk. At this time, I'm not doing any interviews. I don't think it would be appropriate, as a sitting judge. There are many facts about the case that remain confidential, and with the ongoing investigation, it would be inappropriate for me to comment." I also requested the media to keep asking for the release of the records. I knew the only way to clear my name, and bring real justice for Kelsey, the general public needed to know what really happened in the courtroom and during the DHS investigation.

The media filmed me getting out of my car and walking at a normal pace to my office. The spin the media placed on these events was that I was hiding. The media unmercifully made attempts to get me to talk regarding Kelsey's case, yet I maintained my ethical obligations and respected the families.

I think the story that shows the mindset of certain reporters involved a reporter who was with Channel Nine News, the Oklahoma City CBS affiliate. This reporter contacted Sharon, who along with her husband, Joe, has been a foster parent in Lincoln County for over 20 years. Sharon had sent an email to this reporter asking the TV station to contact her. The reporter, in an attempt to dig up some dirt on me, immediately returned Sharon's call. Sharon began defending me. The reporter informed Sharon she was looking for negative stories about my ability as a judge. Sharon told her, "You don't understand. I don't have dirt on Judge Key. You need to say the truth about him." Sharon went through how I had helped three foster children in their care. After being removed from their parents, these children were having difficulty with their school work. I sat the children down, we worked together, and as a result, their grades improved to the point that they were now passing every class. Sharon had seen this happen for several foster kids she'd had in her care since I took the bench. Sharon had seen three judges in our county since she started as a foster parent and she voiced to the reporter how I was the best judge ever, in her opinion.

The reporter told Sharon, "That's not what we're looking for. We don't need any of the good stuff, but if we need anything like that, we'll call you back. I don't need to do a story like that on Judge Key."

It's amazing that the reporter expressed how she was not looking for a story like that on me. Guess what she wanted?

The media learned of my involvement with Youth and Family Resources, Inc. Part of what Youth and Family does is to contract with Eastern Oklahoma Services, Inc. so that CHBS services are provided in Lincoln County.

Several stories were reported regarding my involvement as a board member on Youth and Family, and the fact that the CHBS worker was a contract employee for that non-profit corporation. It is impossible to tie my involvement on that board with any personal knowledge of the CHBS worker, or her involvement with Kelsey.

In addition to the CHBS worker, they also tried to tie the CASA worker to me because that service is also provided under the umbrella of Youth and Family Resources, Inc. As a board member, you do not have knowledge of the day-to-day workings of the organization. No story was off limits, no matter how far fetched it was.

In the second or third week after Kelsey's death, I got a call from *The Daily Oklahoman.* I was informed that the press was looking for any possible tie to the Smith family that might show an improper bias in this case.

I stated that I don't know either one of these families at all. I had never met any member of either family prior to the hearings involving visitation and guardianship of Kelsey.

Ultimately, *The Daily Oklahoman* found out that the CHBS worker on Kelsey's case was a former client of mine. I had represented her years before when her unruly teenage daughter had hit the CHBS worker. The worker grabbed her daughter's hair, took her down, and spanked her with a flyswatter. This was a 16-year-old, two hundred pound girl. Some friend of her daughter's was helping her beat on the CHBS worker.

The Daily Oklahoman made copies of this and called me on a Wednesday to let me know they had found it and to see if I wanted to comment and said they were probably going to run the story on Saturday. Low and behold when they made a copy, the Channel Four reporter, who had visited our county fair, had a spy in the court clerk's office. All of a sudden, *The Daily Oklahoman* made copies of this file and the spy called the Channel Four reporter, who rushed down at 4:15pm, got copies of it, and sensationalized it like I had represented the CHBS worker when she beat her three-year-old daughter. It was an absolute lie.

Channel Four ran the story at 10pm. I had already called the CHBS worker and told her, "Here is what they found." The CHBS worker, who was extremely distraught over the loss of Kelsey, was crying.

The next day I saw her standing outside her car at the drug store on Main Street in Chandler. I told her that she needed to have her daughter set the record straight.

Ultimately, her daughter called the newspaper and cleared up the misunderstanding. That's how the story came about in *The Daily Oklahoman*. They reported the TRUE story. This shows the absolute sensationalism with which some television stations were attacking this. It was sweeps month. They had the number one story, and at this point, people couldn't get enough of it. They were running anything to get ratings.

Finally, it would have been early November, 2005, and I was out at the farm checking cows. I had a bad attitude, and the cold November wind was sweeping across the pasture. My cell phone rang from a number I did not recognize. I answered the phone, ready to pounce on a reporter, when Judge Bartheld of Pittsburgh County, said, "Hello?" (Judge Bartheld was the judge who made the decision in the Ryan Luke case. See the appendix.)

I paused for a moment and he asked, "Is this Judge Key?" I barked, "It is." He said, "This is Judge Bartheld down in Pittsburgh County. I made the Ryan Luke decision. I just want to say welcome to the club, and it's just me and you. I know just how you feel right now." Guess what? He knew!

That's the way it was. It was just the two of us who had gone through this. He began relating his stories of all the pressure he took and ultimately a grand jury investigation cleared him. The grand jury found that he did nothing wrong. But unfortunately, in this case, we never had the grand jury investigation where all of the transcripts could have come out in this case. If we had, the people would have actually known the circumstances that led to my decision.

Judge Bartheld told me that Justice Steven Taylor, the District Court Judge, who is now on the Supreme Court, had asked Judge Bartheld to come up whenever they read the grand jury's findings. He said they read the findings that in fact he was an advocate for children and had done nothing wrong. This was after Governor Frank Keating had come out and demanded Judge Bartheld resign from the bench. But the grand jury, who heard all the testimony in the Ryan Luke case, found that Judge Bartheld was a friend to children, he had done nothing wrong, and he was an advocate for children.

As each one of the Grand Jurors walked past Judge Bartheld, they shook his hand if they were a man and hugged him if they were a woman and said how sorry they were for the heat he had taken, because he had done nothing wrong. The amazing part of this story is that no one reported this finding, except the local newspaper in McAlister, Oklahoma.

The reason I'm sharing this information is not only because of the similarities between the cases, but also because legislation was passed after that case where sealed court documents were to be released to the public. If the transcripts, like I've pushed for all along, had been released, the truth would have already been made public and reform would be taking place that will actually protect children from abusive situations.

The most interesting article, regarding changes in the law, following the Ryan Luke case was demonstrated in the *Shawnee News-Star's* November 13, 2005 article that was titled "Kelsey's records sought under the Ryan Luke Law." According to the article, a child advocate, who had contributed to the writing of the Ryan Luke child abuse law in 1995, fought for the release of Kelsey's records under Ryan's law.

The child advocate explained to *The News-Star* her concern that the law she helped to pass was to protect Oklahoma children. She asked for the release of all of the court documents, so that it could be determined if DHS had indeed failed to protect Kelsey. The Ryan Luke Law states that transcripts are to be released to the public within seven days. She stated, "I'm doing my best working with the media to interpret the Ryan Luke Law as it exists and was intended."

This child advocate echoed my sentiment that the court records and DHS documents should be publicized. At the time this article was published, the transcripts had not yet been typed. At the time of this article, it was hoped that the transcripts would soon be released. They still haven't been to this day.

This child advocate said, "DHS did not recommend the child be placed with her mother. That says to me that DHS did their job." Yes, the DHS did their job by asking that Kelsey be slowly integrated back into her home, and for workers to keep a close eye on her in the days after her reunion with her mother, but they didn't ask that Kelsey not be returned to her home at all, which is a common misconception.

She further stated, "The child has already paid the price. But if we can make the system better, that's what needs to be done."[1] I'm in total agreement with this statement. That is the reason for this book...

On the Thursday after Kelsey's death, I wanted to "rally the troops," regroup, and focus on the children that we still were there to help. To do this, I sat down with the DA and the DHS and told them, "We have to raise the level of our game." It was at that point we changed a couple of things. The DA's office and DHS were not staffing every week like they're supposed to. They were not meeting to discuss the cases before they were heard in court. That creates an enormous problem when the DA and the DHS are not discussing the facts of the cases and aren't on the same page of where they are going.

Afterthought

Hopefully this book will bring to light the facts in this one-sided media assault in this deadly game of tug-of-war and instigate a change by the legislature requiring the release of court records after the untimely death of a child in DHS custody. The problem remains that until the records are released, the media must search for unknown facts in an effort to tell the child's story.

---

[1] Shawnee News Star Web-Posted Nov. 13, 2005 02:01: AM ,
http://www.news-star.com/stories/111305/new_20051113063.shtml

CHAPTER SIXTEEN

Campaign for Re-election

In January, 2006, *The Daily Oklahoman* ran an article announcing my intentions to run for re-election. I never doubted my intention to put in a bid to extend my term on the bench. If I had felt I had done something wrong in Kelsey's case, I would have resigned months before the 2006 election.

However, I felt the key to winning the election was to get the legislation to agree to the release of all the confidential records such as the court transcripts and DHS records that existed before and after Kelsey's death. Throughout the winter I lobbied hard for the legislature to release the court and DHS records. I knew the only way to defend myself against any possible attacks on my character or my ability as a judge was with those records. Without the records, the mischaracterization of the testimony and evidence could seemingly go on forever. I also knew how ugly the campaign would become would depend on the ethical values of the candidate who would run against me. All attorneys, and particularly judges, know you cannot look at one decision and use the outcome of that decision as proof of a judge's ability. This is especially true when the records are sealed to the public, and all candidates cannot openly discuss the case.

It was now May, 2006, and I was waiting on someone to step-up and announce their candidacy. Rumors were flying, and I just concentrated on getting my message ready to deliver to the people of Lincoln County, Oklahoma. Since being elected in 2002, I had delivered on every campaign promise I made. The Lincoln County Drug Court was having a success rate of over 85%. That means that over 8 out of every 10 people that entered drug court not only graduated, but stayed clean months afterward.

Community service hours for criminal defendants were in excess of 30,000 hours in the four years I was judge. Project Safe had set up an office to help victims of domestic violence. An accountability program for criminal offenders, and paid for without tax dollars, had been established as well. I was excited for people to see what we had accomplished during my term, but I did not realize the unethical depths my opponent would sink to in this election.

It was mid-May when Sheila Kirk came into my office. She told me she had decided to run against me, and I told her that I was looking forward to the race. I'll never forget her looking me in the eyes and shaking my extended hand, as she guaranteed that the name "Kelsey Smith-Briggs" would never come out of her mouth during the campaign.

Sheila's guarantee was short-lived. From the beginning of the campaign, to its end, the woman Sheila Kirk called "white trash" that day in my office joined forces with her as political allies. The pair would go door-to-door across the county, as well as to senior citizen centers and other events, telling people that I was the one responsible for the death of Kelsey Smith-Briggs.

The first event I had to deal with as the campaign kicked off was the Chandler Alumni Parade. Kathie called the alumni President and said that, according to Kathie, her organization would be participating in the alumni parade. They wanted to hand out literature that basically called me a "baby killer."

The alumni association denied her access at the parade, but it was clear what the tone of the election was going to be from that point forward. The judicial ethics, by which I was governed, and the upcoming Michael Porter trial prohibited my ability to comment on the specifics of Kelsey's case. I would be unable to go on the defensive against the campaign that was being launched, not for Sheila Kirk as judge, but against me as the judge who returned Kelsey to her mother.

To add to the turmoil that was erupting, Kathie Briggs' website and forum asked for help to ensure that I was not re-elected. On her forum, in the comments section, her supporters wrote things like, "A lot of us do not live in Lincoln County but we can still help campaign. I don't care what she (Sheila Kirk) stands for. I would be campaigning against Judge Key. We know what he stands for and you couldn't vote in a worse judge than that. I can't believe he has the guts to get out there and campaign. He has been in hiding since October 11, 2005." and "So Kathie, I have never had anything to do with a political campaign before so I know nothing about them. Please tell me what I need to do, when and where."

A former DHS worker, who had been a regular on Kathie's website, knew Sheila Kirk, and had worked with her during her time as an Assistant District Attorney, posted a different thought – "I am sorry, I cannot support Sheila Kirk for a judge's position. I was the Child Welfare Supervisor for Lincoln County when she was Assistant DA under Miles Zimmerman. She handled all CW (child welfare) cases in Lincoln Co. and in my opinion, was a total disaster. She was unprofessional, bordered on incompetent, and didn't do what was in the best interests of the children. She tended to take the path of the least resistance and do what was the easiest or the least amount of effort for her. She refused to file on many cases, especially sexual abuse cases. And if she did file the CW case, she wouldn't file criminal charges. So a lot of abusers and molesters in this county walked off 'Scott free' because of her. It made CW's job nearly impossible. I never felt that she cared about the children. It was just a part of her job that was the biggest nuisance that she had to do to get the paycheck. I never felt that she understood the purpose of CW or understood the law in general. The judge we had at the time seemed to despise her because she made so many dumb mistakes over and over. Other attorneys ridiculed her because of her poor performance in the courtroom as well. I believe much of this was that she didn't care and didn't prepare, which is unforgivable for an attorney, especially in a CW case. Also, she was fired immediately when Kaye Christiansen, who was a strong child advocate, became DA after Zimmerman was fired. She may have changed in the last 10 years, but without some very convincing proof, I won't support her. Just my opinion."

During my campaign, I focused solely on the positive changes that had occurred in our county. I knew that during my time on the bench the programs I helped implement had made a difference. There were still changes and improvements that I wanted to make as I continued to serve the public. For example, across the street from the courthouse is a small, white house. In early 2004, well over a year before Kelsey's death, I made an agreement with a local attorney, who owned the house, to turn it into the Partney House. It would have been a multi-function facility from which we could ultimately have juveniles testify without having to look at their abusers in the courtroom. This also would have allowed abused and neglected children to sit in the house, rather than wait in the sterile environment of the courthouse hallways before they testified. It would have also provided a place for parents and children to interact and have supervised visitation before and after court.

As all the criticism over Kelsey was in full swing, I decided to use this as an opportunity to create the best possible facilities to deal with juveniles. In February, 2006, David, the DHS supervisor and I went out to El Reno to see what Judge Miller has created. He has the best programs and the best facilities in the State of Oklahoma. Among his facilities, is a self-contained courthouse, including a courtroom, court clerk's office, alternative school, juvenile detention center, on-staff psychologist, counseling services for parents and children, everything all-in-one.

I knew we could not create exactly what Judge Miller has in El Reno, but my goal was to maximize our affiliation with the Sac and Fox Indian tribe, which already has a juvenile detention center, and by using the Part-ney House, along with other resources, we could come close.

I went to Richard Smotherman, the District Attorney, and asked him to explain my vision for the children of Lincoln County to Kathie Briggs. My goal was to create a courtroom in Kelsey's honor, and to be progressive in our approach to juveniles.

Smotherman informed me that Kathie Briggs did not wish to discuss any improvements to our facilities in Lincoln County if it meant dealing with me.

I have read where Kathie stated that I never contacted her. However, every time I attempted to reach out to her, it was met with a negative response.

It was now August, 2006, and at the Lincoln County Free Fair in Chandler I had a booth. Just as in other rural counties, the annual county fair is a big deal. Hundreds of children exhibit animals, produce, or crafts and everyone shows up to participate as a family event.

I ran an ad in the paper telling people they could come ask me about the Kelsey case. The ad read: "Within judicial and ethical limits find out all the facts possible about this case." It was my desire to allow the voters of Lincoln County a chance to ask any question they had involving Kelsey's case.

I was gone from the booth when a reporter for KFOR, Channel Four, the NBC affiliate out of Oklahoma City, showed up and verbally attacked the gentleman and his wife who were working at my booth. The reporter came there to attack me. They were basically just looking to try and force me to talk with a complete disregard for the citizens at the fair.

I wasn't there, so this reporter got into a verbal altercation with the gentleman and his wife who were working my booth. As my associate walked away from them, the cameraman bumped him with his camera. My associate told the cameraman to remove the camera from his face.

It was at this point that the cameraman loudly proclaimed my associate to be a "backwards country jackass." He said this in front of women, children, and everyone who was there within our county fair. There was a lady who works at the USDA county extension office, was sitting with her seven-year-old twin daughters right next to this confrontation. In addition, a lady who was working the Farm Bureau booth, plus all sorts of other individuals witnessed the event. The cameraman had no regard for our little county fair, nor did he have any respect for our citizens.

Instead, they wanted to come down and verbally and physically assault me and my people in order to get their story.

During this time, newspaper ads, ran by Sheila Kirk, were distorting the facts of Kelsey's case. The attorney for Kelsey decided to set the record straight, and sent the following letter on September 21, 2006, to the editors of both the *Lincoln County News* and the *Stroud American.* Both papers ran the letter he sent as follows:

"To the Editor,

As the attorney for Kelsey Smith-Briggs, I am writing this letter to set the record straight regarding several issues pertaining to Kelsey's case. Unfortunately, her death has become a political football and it concerns me that some are pointing fingers without having full knowledge of the facts.

Whether you support Judge Craig Key or his opponent, Sheila Kirk, I would encourage everyone to base their decision on the truth rather than emotion. To do otherwise would not serve the voters and citizens of this county. The truth is Judge Key had the legal obligation to return Kelsey to her mother. The Court, as well as myself, were advised that the mother had completed the Individualized Service Plan created for her by the Department of Human Services (DHS), and there were no additional requirements of her. The Oklahoma legislature has declared that it is the official public policy of this state to reunite children with their parents under such circumstances.

The truth is that Kelsey's placement with her mother in June of last year was conditioned upon the stipulation and Court order that there would be significant monitoring by various child welfare agencies. That is exactly what happened. The truth is that during the four months that Kelsey was in the care of her mother, none of those responsible for overseeing Kelsey's well-being ever reported to me or the Court that there were any problems with the care she was receiving. The truth is no one ever objected to or appealed Judge Key's ruling to return Kelsey to her mother.

Based upon the evidence presented to the Court, and the monitoring and oversight requirement that was put in place on behalf of Kelsey, I do not believe that at that point in time any of the parties involved in the case feared for her safety, much less, her life.

No one has a crystal ball or can foretell the future. Judges and lawyers rely on the law and evidence. Everyone knows this. The more Kelsey's tragic situation is exploited and politicized, we will only move farther from the truth of what really happened to Kelsey. The people of Lincoln County should not be pulled apart or deceived by this sad incident. Sincerely, ... Attorney for Kelsey Smith-Briggs"

The campaign was coming to a close, and I anticipated extreme negative campaigning from my opponent. The last two tricks used by Sheila were more than I could have imagined.

In late October, Sheila did a direct mailing, showing Lance Briggs in his military uniform, looking down on Kelsey. It proclaimed that Kelsey was killed while Lance fought for our freedom. The mail-out also described how Lance walked off the military transport plane to learn that

Kelsey had died that day, and proclaiming that I should not be re-elected because of my failure to protect Kelsey.

Finally, when Sheila Kirk had Kathie Briggs call every voter in the county several times with the following pre-recorded message, it was a new low. The message left by Kathie Briggs was as follows:

"My name is Kathie Briggs, and I am the paternal grandmother of Kelsey Briggs, who died after months of documented abuse. Judge Craig Key returned her (Kelsey) to an abusive home against the recommendation of DHS and the DA's office. Judge Key also broke Oklahoma law, which requires DHS, not him, to make those decisions. I promised Kelsey I would seek to hold those who failed her accountable. I ask you to help me, to keep that promise. Please vote for Sheila Kirk, Associate District Judge on November 7th. If you have any questions, please contact Sheila Kirk at 405-258-2300. Thank you and God bless."

These phone messages attempted to emotionally inflame the voters, without providing a positive reason to elect Sheila Kirk.

On November 7, 2006, I lost my bid for re-election. As I previously stated, at the beginning of the book, my family has resided, worked, and raised several generations of children in Chandler, Oklahoma. The only saving grace for me personally, from the election, is the fact that Chandler voted overwhelmingly for me to retain my position as Associate District Judge of Lincoln County.

As irony would have it, the sun rose on November 8, 2006, and I, once again, forced myself to go to work. At the end of the day, I returned to my farm to check on my cattle. As I eased my way down the drive of my farm, walking out from behind a grove of scrub oak trees was the number 13 cow, with a new calf, born the day before.

Afterthought

The reason I included this chapter is because it shows what happens when a judicial candidate with little or no ethical limits is able to take advantage of a sitting judge's decision, when the court transcripts, documents, or DHS records have not been released to the public. Kelsey's case is an emotionally charged issue that was wielded like a club against the constituents of Lincoln County as the reason I should not be re-elected without a positive reason to elect my opponent.

A Deadly Game of Tug of War

CHAPTER SEVENTEEN

Ongoing Investigations

I've been asked on several occasions to play Monday morning quarterback and reevaluate the case with the facts that I have learned since Kelsey's death, in order to determine if I would have made the same decision. That is something that I, unfortunately, am unable to do. There are only two people who know what happened on that fateful day in October; one is no longer with us, and the other holds a secret that must be slowly killing him or her with guilt that is too much for anyone to bear.

A precious baby, child, daughter, granddaughter, great-granddaughter, niece, cousin, step-sister, step-daughter, however you choose to refer to Kelsey, this precious little girl has lost her life at the hands of an unknown assailant. The perpetrator will never be known, or prosecuted for Kelsey's murder. Some aspects of this case are still being heard in Oklahoma courts today, as Kelsey's mother is set to stand trial for either enabling child abuse or actually abusing Kelsey.

As far as I knew, Kelsey's placement back into her mother's home was going fine. But it became apparent to the Smith family soon after Kelsey's return home to Raye Dawn in June, 2005, that Michael Porter wasn't the knight in shining armor Raye Dawn thought he was. He became controlling, jealous, and sinking deep into a financial hole, which his family was unaware of at the time.

Porter owned a house in Shawnee where the couple lived after their wedding, until they moved into a home in Meeker, Oklahoma that they had purchased from Gayla Smith; the same home Kelsey lived in during her final days.

Not long after the couple moved into their new home in Meeker, Porter's home in Shawnee was foreclosed and his automobile was repossessed. *What would cause a man who seemed to have it all to lose everything so quickly?* He appeared to be weaving a tangled web of lies. When Raye Dawn met Porter, he claimed to have graduated from Oklahoma State University (this was untrue) and appeared to be earning a good living.

Yet, Porter changed the week they closed on their home in Meeker, which was the Wednesday before Kelsey died. It was as if he had snapped and wasn't the same person at all those last few days. During that same time, Porter would say to Raye Dawn, "I hate you sometimes." *They were newlyweds!*

On October 20, 2005, Michael Porter was arrested for the murder of Kelsey Smith-Briggs. The Oklahoma Medical Examiner's Office ruled Kelsey's death a homicide, and that she died from blunt force trauma to the abdomen.

The debate raged for months regarding who was responsible for the murder of little Kelsey. Kathie Briggs began a campaign to have Raye Dawn Smith charged with enabling child abuse. By this time, the media storm was in full force, and the public had been convinced Kelsey had been abused, and that everyone turned a blind eye to the abuse.

Kathie Briggs and her supporters picketed the office of Richard Smotherman, the District Attorney, until the political pressure grew so strong that on February 24, 2006, criminal charges were filed against Kelsey's mother, Raye Dawn Smith.

From February, 2006, until Michael Porter's preliminary hearing on August 23, 2006, the D.A. and Raye Dawn's attorney attempted to negotiate a plea bargain for Kelsey's mother. The D.A. knew without Raye Dawn placing Kelsey alive at the house when Porter showed up on the afternoon of October 11, 2005, he had no case. Ultimately, Raye Dawn agreed to testify at Porter's preliminary hearing, without a plea bargain.

During this time, the D.A. hired an Indiana expert to perform an additional autopsy on Kelsey. At the request of the D.A., Kelsey's body was exhumed from the Meeker, Oklahoma cemetery. I was told by a member of the D.A.'s office that this autopsy found Kelsey had suffered a pancreatic injury that could be consistent with an injury suffered in the auto accident on August 19, 2005.

According to this source, the Indiana doctor found that Kelsey had also been sexually abused, and it was likely to have occurred on the day of her death. Under this doctor's theory, Kelsey had reacted, as a result of the sexual abuse, rupturing a vein in her pancreas and causing her to bleed to death internally.

On August 23, 2006, the media circled the Lincoln County Courthouse. The news stations had a live feed truck located on every corner, and newspaper photographers camped outside, waiting for a chance to snap a picture of any participant in the hearing.

At the hearing, Raye Dawn testified that she had never seen Porter physically abuse Kelsey. On the afternoon of October 11, 2005, Kelsey had an accident and urinated in her panties before her nap. Raye Dawn had put her to bed without any panties or pull-up on, but when she got to the ambulance, Porter had placed a diaper on Kelsey before the paramedics arrived.

At the conclusion of the preliminary hearing, Porter was bound over for trial for the crimes of murder in the first degree and sexual abuse of a child. His trial was set for February, 2007. It was during this time that the attorney for Porter learned he had corresponded with the Briggs after Kelsey's death.

On February 2, 2007, the District Attorney, Richard Smotherman, discussed the first degree murder and sexual abuse of a child charges with Porter's attorney. Porter's attorney and the D.A. struck a plea bargain that meant no one would ever be prosecuted for Kelsey's murder. Pursuant to the plea bargain, Porter was convicted of enabling child abuse by not reporting that he saw Raye Dawn strike Kelsey in the stomach in July, 2005.

Now, Porter became a witness and is going to testify against Raye Dawn at her trial.

It is my belief that this injustice occurred because of the deadly tug-of-war between a mother, a grandmother, a father with a history of domestic abuse, and a step-father who wanted attention from his new bride.

Does Raye Dawn have hope of receiving a fair trial in our state? Newslink, the closed captioning service for local television channels 4, 5, 9, 13, and 25 has reported that to date they have transcripts of 910 stories on this case since Kelsey's death in October of 2005. This is equivalent to almost two stories reported per day since this case started. The local newspaper, *The Daily Oklahoman*, has produced on its online version Newsok. com, 59 stories about Kelsey. The *Shawnee News-Star* has produced 62 articles in print and on their website in the same timeframe.

Not only has the media had a field day, but there are websites filled with accusations against Raye Dawn.

The paternal family has spearheaded an organization to produce billboards, rallies, hundreds of fliers, and thousands of bumper stickers and buttons that feature Kelsey's picture and claim that Kelsey's purpose on this earth was to die so that other children can be protected.

A local television station, Fox 25, took a poll that asked "Do you think Raye Dawn Smith can get a fair trail in Lincoln County?" An overwhelming response showed that 79% of those who answered the poll voted "No."

On February 3, 2007, the Briggs told a reporter with *Shawnee News-Star*, "The Kelsey we remembered felt love and safe while in our care... Up to now, Michael Porter is the only one that has personally expressed his remorse to me and is now taking responsibility...He's the only person that has stepped up and taken a very serious punishment for his LIMITED involvement in the death of Kelsey."

Afterthought

The final chapter of this saga is yet to be written as the trial of Raye Dawn Smith will take place after the publication of this book. However, this book is a timeless example of the damage done when two families forget about the child in their pursuit to punish the other family.

A Deadly Game of Tug of War

CHAPTER EIGHTEEN

Reflections

While there are many people who have been hurt by the outcome of this case, the only true victim was Kelsey.

There has not been a single day since October 11, 2005 that my mind has not drifted back to her captivating smile, twinkling blue eyes, and golden locks of hair. When I think of Kelsey, I envision her dancing in the courthouse lobby, just as she did

> While there are many people who have been hurt by the outcome of this case, the only true victim was Kelsey.

that late afternoon in June, 2005. It's an image that will be forever burned in my memory, and it is that image which motivated me to tell Kelsey's difficult and heart wrenching story.

To be able to convey an accurate account of the events surrounding Kelsey's life and death, I have spent the past few months assembling and pouring over all the information from this case. It has been a difficult process, and I would not be human if I did not ask the question "what if?"

My frustration over the loss of Kelsey is an inability to pinpoint the breakdown in the legal system, the child welfare system, or her family in order to prevent such tragedies in the future. My conclusion is that the best decision made from the information provided by family members and concerned agencies and authorities can still result in tragic consequences. Would you have made the same decision?

You have now taken the time to read about Kelsey's painful life and tragic end. Please take a moment and answer these questions:

- Based on the timeline (located in the appendix) from January, 2005, to the testimony and evidence of the bruises to Kelsey's buttocks presented at the February 4, 2005 hearing, do you believe guardianship should have been granted to Kathie Briggs?

- Were the broken collarbone and facial bruising Kelsey suffered in January, 2005 accidental injuries, as the Meeker Police Department and DHS determined, or intentional child abuse?

- Were the March 24, 2005 bruised nose and knee that Kelsey suffered while at her mother's apartment a result of a normal childhood accident?

- In April, 2005, the parties changed the visitation schedule on their own, and Kelsey bounced between her mother's and grandmother's homes. During this time, two different doctors diagnosed Kelsey with broken legs. One doctor said child abuse, the other said accidental injury. Which doctor was correct in his or her diagnosis? In whose care did the breaks occur?

- You have learned how Kelsey reacted to both her mother and paternal grandmother during supervised visits from May, 2005 to June 15, 2005. With your knowledge of the case during that period, where would you place Kelsey at the end of the hearing that was held on June 16, 2005?

- At the September 8, 2005 hearing, nearly three months after Kelsey was returned to her mother's care, the Assistant District Attorney and Kelsey's attorney moved to dismiss the case. The paternal side of the family was not present for the hearing. Can you find any reason to remove Kelsey from her mother's custody at that point?

Your answers were given with a glimpse into the future, and you know the outcome of this case. I made every one of these decisions without hindsight or a crystal ball to see into the future. At the time each decision was made, I did so to the best of my ability, given the information provided to me. Judges are human, and when you are making decisions like these, the black robe feels like it weighs a thousand pounds.

The changes that need to be made, as a result of Kelsey's case and hundreds like hers across the country, are not only to the legal system, but also to family structures. In the appendix, I suggest changes to our legal and child welfare systems, but we must first examine what changes are necessary in order to once again have families be responsible for their own children. As a society, we must look at how we fail our children, before we can criticize how the system fails.

A Deadly Game of Tug of War

APPENDIX

The Timeline

It is important to understand the timeline of the events that occurred once the Court, DHS, and other parties got involved in the private lives of Kelsey Smith-Briggs and her family.

Most of the events leading up to Kelsey's untimely death occurred between January and October of 2005. It seemed that most of Kelsey's bruising and injuries occurred while in the care of Raye Dawn Smith and Michael Porter, but the Department of Human Services ultimately found that the abuse could have taken place in the Smith-Porter home as well as the Briggs home because Kathie and Royce Briggs had primary custody of Kelsey from February until May. In fact, most of the worst injuries occurred during the time Kelsey was shuffled between homes.

Following is a sequence of events as they occurred during the months in question:

Some time in late 2004 the Smith family was informed by a person who was closely related to both the Smith and Briggs family, that Raye Dawn Smith and her family had better get ready for a bitter custody battle.

January 8, 2005 – Kelsey suffers a broken collarbone and bruises to her face while in care of Raye Dawn Smith.

January 10, 2005 – Raye Dawn takes Kelsey to the emergency room in Shawnee, Oklahoma. The doctors diagnose Kelsey with a broken clavicle (collarbone) and observe scratches to her neck and arm.

January 13, 2005 – Raye Dawn and Kelsey spend the night with Gayla Smith.

January 14, 2005 – Raye Dawn picks up Kelsey from her day-care at 5pm and takes her to Kathie Briggs at 6pm.

January 14, 2005 at 11pm – Lance and Ashley Briggs, Kelsey's father and step-mother, take Kelsey to the emergency room in Shawnee, Oklahoma where Kelsey has bruises to her buttocks and the side of her face.

January 16, 2005 – Kathie refuses to return Kelsey to Raye Dawn and keeps her overnight.

January 17, 2005 – Raye Dawn goes to the Meeker police to report Kathie's refusal to return Kelsey. The police make Kathie return Kelsey to Raye Dawn.

January 19, 2005 – takes custody of Kelsey because DHS has concerns about the bruising.

January 21, 2005 – Raye Dawn Smith takes Kelsey to doctor to find out why she bruises easily.

January 24, 2005 – Royce and Kathie Briggs apply for emergency guardianship. I sign a custody order granting emergency temporary custody to the Briggs. Kathie Briggs goes to Kelsey's daycare with the police and takes immediate custody of Kelsey.

February 4, 2005 – I conduct a trial on the guardianship to determine if Kathie and Royce Briggs should remain guardians of Kelsey. Based on the statements of DHS and other facts, which will be discussed in detail later in the book, I leave Kelsey in the temporary custody of the Briggs and grant Raye Dawn supervised visitation.

February 11, 2005 – Case had been continued to this date to allow DHS to complete investigation. DA's office asks for 30 days to file deprived petition, the hearing is continued to March 11, 2005.

February 23, 2005 – DA files their petition seeking to have Kelsey adjudicated deprived.

March 11, 2005 – Parties meet for the continued hearing and the case is continued to June 6th with the guardianship and deprived cases consolidated to be heard jointly.

March 11, 2005 – After court, DHS meets with Raye Dawn, her attorney, Greg Wilson, and Kelsey's court appointed attorney where she is advised of the classes she must complete to have Kelsey returned.

March 24, 2005 – Kelsey suffers a bruise on her nose and right knee after a fall while visiting Raye Dawn Smith at her Meeker apartment.

March 24, 2005 - Kathie and Ashley Briggs take Kelsey to the emergency room to have the injuries documented for DHS. The Briggs tell ER personnel they believe Raye Dawn's story of Kelsey falling, but just want the bruise documented for the custody case.

March 31, 2005 – Kelsey's hair starts falling out to the point that she has a bald spot the size of a baseball and she starts self-mutilating by biting herself while in the custody of Kathie Briggs.

April 14, 2005 – Kelsey suffers a sprained ankle while at the zoo with Raye Dawn Smith's sister-in-law, Miste. Raye Dawn and Miste take Kelsey to the emergency room where her ankle is X-rayed and she is diagnosed with a sprained ankle. (Allegedly, Kathie later stated that Miste should be charged with child abuse because Kelsey was in Miste's care when she fell at the zoo.)

April 15, 2005 – Kelsey suffers bruising to both thighs and bruising to her rib-cage after falling through screen door while at friend's house in care of Michael Porter.

April 18, 2005 – Raye Dawn Smith marries Michael Porter.

April 19 – 21, 2005 – Kelsey is in the home of Kathie Briggs. Raye Dawn takes Kelsey to DHS to report that Kelsey is not walking. Some time later, when questioned about the injury, Kathie tells DHS that Kelsey took four steps on April 19, 2005, but never walked again while in her care. Kathie never contacted anyone or took Kelsey to a doctor after she quit walking. Why?

April 25, 2005 – Kelsey is in the care of Raye Dawn, who notices the leg Kelsey did not injure is swollen and hot to the touch. She takes Kelsey to the DHS office in Lincoln County and is advised by workers and DHS's nurse to immediately take Kelsey to the emergency room. Dr. Barrett, an orthopedic specialist in Shawnee, diagnoses Kelsey with two broken legs.

April 26, 2005 – Dr. Barrett places casts on both of Kelsey's legs.

April 27, 2005 – Kelsey suffers a bruise to her nose and eyebrow from her step-sister elbowing her in bed while in the care of Raye Dawn Smith and Michael Porter.

May 2, 2005 – Kathie takes Kelsey to OU Medical Center in Oklahoma City for a second opinion on Kelsey's broken legs. Dr. Sullivan, an orthopedic specialist, determines Kelsey's legs may have been broken by non-accidental trauma.

May 3, 2005 – The District Attorney's office, at the request of DHS asks that I place Kelsey in protective custody when they determine that both Kathie Briggs and Raye Dawn Smith are suspects to the alleged abuse. Kelsey is placed in the care of Gayla Smith, her maternal grandmother, by DHS.

May 5, 2005 – Raye Dawn's attorney files an application to terminate the Briggs' guardianship. I conduct a "show cause" hearing and leave legal custody of Kelsey with DHS. Both Raye Dawn and the Briggs are granted four hours of visitation per week, with visitation to occur at and be supervised by DHS. The next hearing is set for June 6, 2005.

May 10, 2005 – I appoint a representative of CASA (Court Appointed Special Advocate) to investigate and represent Kelsey's interest.

May 11, 2005 – The District Attorney's office files an amended petition and changes the allegations in their February 23, 2005 petition. The amended petition alleges:

"The Respondent Juvenile has been physically abused as evidenced by her two broken legs. The respondents, mother and paternal grandmother either perpetrated the acts of abuse or failed to protect the respondent juvenile from the abuse."

May 12, 2005 – CASA worker contacts DHS and begins reviewing all allegations and DHS files plus court files in order to prepare court report for June hearing.

May 31, 2005 – DHS goes over mother's Individualized Service Plan and addresses risk factors within the mother's home, as identified by DHS.

June 1, 2005 – DHS recommends Community Home Based Services (CHBS) be placed in mother's home upon child's return to provide better supervision and improve parenting skills so that Kelsey will not sustain any other injuries.

June 1, 2005 – CASA report filed with the Court. CASA recommends:

- Kelsey be returned to her mother's custody
- The paternal grandparents can have supervised visitation one hour every other Saturday
- Kelsey can spend time at the maternal grandmother's home, including spending the night

- If this arrangement does not work out, Kelsey was to be placed in the maternal grandmother's home until the court decides otherwise

- Kelsey should be enrolled in Head Start and have a speech therapist help her with her language

- A request for a 90-day review, due to "having this case such a short time"

June 3, 2005 – Lincoln County District Attorney's office files a motion for continuance to allow DHS additional time to complete their report.

June 6, 2005 – Referral made to DHS by unknown caller alleging neglect of Michael Porter's children, Kelsey's step-brother and step-sister. This referral was "screened out" due to the fact the caller could not provide names of anyone who would have seen the abuse.

June 6, 2005 – I continued the court hearing after having all attorneys and DHS in my chambers. I ordered the DHS report to be filed by the close of business on June 10, 2005, and set the hearing on the guardianship and the amended deprived petition for June 14, 2005. I told all attorneys in my chambers the time had come to try this case.

June 15 – 16, 2005 – The trial was conducted as to the guardianship filed by the Briggs and the amended deprived petition filed by the DA's office. The testimony and evidence presented at this 12-hour hearing will be gone through in detail later. Ultimately, I returned Kelsey to her mother at the conclusion of the hearing.

June 20, 2005 – Raye Dawn contacts DHS to let them know Kelsey is doing fine. Raye Dawn takes Kelsey to the zoo, swimming, and has a cookout with her family during this time.

June 27, 2005 – Raye Dawn calls DHS to let them know Kelsey is doing fine. Kelsey asks and is allowed to talk to the worker.

Kelsey's hair continues to grow back and she is eating well, but is suffering from possible separation anxiety when she lays down for her nap. According to DHS, Kelsey fears Raye Dawn will not be there when she wakes up.

June 30, 2005 – DHS contacts Ashley Briggs to set up visit. Ashley advises DHS that Kathie told her visitation was not allowed with their side of the family. DHS advises Ashley that this is incorrect and sets up visitation for July 6, 2005.

July 2, 2005 – DHS makes regular visit to Raye Dawn Smith's home, everything is going fine.

July 7, 2005 – First visit from CHBS worker, who is with DHS worker. They observe Raye Dawn being very attentive to both Kelsey and Kelsey's step-sister. All interaction between the family members was "very normal and appropriate."

July 8, 2005 – CASA worker visits Kelsey and Raye Dawn at their home.

July 12, 2005 – CASA report filed recommending:

- That Kelsey stay with her mother
- That the biological father and stepmother have one hour of supervised visitation every 30 days, or as determined by DHS
- That Kelsey can spend the night with the maternal grandmother
- That the mother had completed her program

July 12, 2005 - I ruled that Kelsey was to remain with Raye Dawn Smith and have overnight visits with her father when he returns to the state.

July 12, 2005 – CHBS visits Raye Dawn and Kelsey at their home.

July 13, 2005 – Ashley Briggs contacts DHS to set up another appointment for visitation with Kelsey. Ashley advises that Kathie gave her the OU physician's medical bill. The bill came to Kathie Briggs' home with Raye Dawn Porter's name on it and wants to get the bill to Raye Dawn. Worker advises Ashley that the Briggs' insurance needs to pay for the bill because the injury occurred before Kelsey was placed in DHS custody.

July 14, 2005 – Raye Dawn and Kelsey met CHBS at Lincoln County Courthouse.

July 18, 2005 – Raye Dawn met CASA at Lincoln County Courthouse.

July 19, 2005 – CHBS visits home of Raye Dawn, Kelsey, and family.

July 20, 2005 – Ashley Briggs contacts DHS worker to have her call Raye Dawn to advise that Lance has been trying to call to speak with Kelsey. DHS worker advises Ashley to have Lance mail letters, cards, or other correspondence to Kelsey. DHS worker encourages Ashley to send pictures, etc to Kelsey. Ashley demands DHS worker advise her about the CHBS program. DHS worker explains that the program is going extremely well and the DHS worker has regular contact with the CHBS worker. Once again, Ashley asks worker about the doctor bill received at Kathie Briggs' home in Raye Dawn's name. Worker advises Ashley that the services provided were before Kelsey went into DHS custody and will have to be paid by Kathie Briggs.

July 20, 2005 – DHS worker contacts Raye Dawn regarding phone calls for Kelsey by her dad, Lance. Raye Dawn advises worker that she has never received a message or phone call from Lance. Raye Dawn agrees that if Lance writes to Kelsey, she will read any cards, letters, etc to her. Raye Dawn advises the DHS worker that Kelsey has gained weight to 24 pounds.

July 25, 2005 – Raye Dawn contacts DHS worker to check in.

July 26, 2005 – CHBS visits Kelsey, Raye Dawn, and family at their home.

August 1, 2005 – Raye Dawn contacts DHS.

August 2, 2005 – CHBS visits Kelsey, Raye Dawn, and family at their home.

August 2, 2005 – Kelsey reportedly is having night terrors and self-mutilating. (This was never reported to me by DHS.)

August 4, 2005 – Kelsey's nose is red and bleeding from sinus problems when DHS visits home. (This was never reported to me by DHS.) DHS asks Raye Dawn to make doctor appointment for Kelsey because of her issues of hurting herself. DHS notes the house is neat and clean and the family appears to be very bonded.

> Raye Dawn brings up the possibility of counseling.

August 5, 2005 – Home visit by DHS. DHS finds Raye Dawn to be very concerned with Kelsey injuring herself. Raye Dawn brings up the possibility of counseling.

August 11, 2005 – CHBS visits Kelsey, Raye Dawn, and family at their home. Kelsey reportedly has had a good week with no more night terrors or self-mutilating. CHBS worker asks Raye Dawn for permission to visit with Oklahoma Commission on Children and Youth (OCCY.) Raye Dawn agrees and states that she appreciates that they are interested in the well-being of Kelsey. CHBS worker explains that Par Post Adjudication Review Board will be held on November 1, 2005, where OCCY, CHBS, CASA, and PARB will have a round-table discussion about Kelsey.

August 16, 2005 – CHBS visits Kelsey, Raye Dawn, and family at their home.

August 16, 2005 - CHBS goes with Raye Dawn for Kelsey's appointment with Dr. Koons regarding her self-inflicted injuries.

August 17, 2005 – CASA report filed with the court recommends:

- Continued placement in the mother and step-father's home

- One hour unsupervised visitation every other Saturday at father and step-mother's home

- Kelsey can spend time at maternal grandmother's home including spending the night

August 18, 2005 – I conduct a further dispositional hearing and grant Ashley additional visitation on alternating weekends beginning August 20, 2005 from 9am to 2pm. These visits are to be unsupervised. If Lance returns home, he shall receive standard visitation every other weekend upon his return. If Kelsey needs any medical attention while in the care of Ashley and/or Lance, they shall immediately notify Raye Dawn.

August 19, 2005 – CHBS visits Kelsey, Raye Dawn, and family at their home.

August 19, 2005 – Kelsey is injured in auto accident in the family vehicle with Raye Dawn Smith and Michael Porter when hit by a drunk driver. Kelsey suffers bruising to her face and unknown internal injuries. Raye Dawn and Porter take Kelsey to the emergency room and leave several hours later, before seeing a physician.

August 23, 2005 – Kelsey starts refusing food.

August 25, 2005 – CHBS visits Kelsey, Raye Dawn, and family at their home.

August 25, 2005 – Raye Dawn takes Kelsey to the doctor, who documents Kelsey's bruises from auto accident.

August 26, 2005 – Kelsey has seizure while in the care of Raye Dawn.

August 29, 2005 – Ashley visits with Kelsey at her and Lance's home. Ashley takes pictures of Kelsey in the swing with Kelsey's bruises from auto accident.

August 29, 2005 – DHS receives a report of allegations of abuse. It states that Kelsey has bruises on her face, a mark on her nose, she appears to have lost weight, and she's acting timid. This report is "screened out" due to the fact that Kelsey's doctor documented the injuries from the auto accident on August 25th.

August 26, 2005 – CHBS visits Kelsey, Raye Dawn, and family at their home.

August 30, 2005 – Raye Dawn takes Kelsey to DHS, who refers Kelsey to the Child Study Center in Oklahoma City for play therapy counseling.

August 30, 2005 – The Court receives a letter from Kelsey's doctor recommending that Kelsey remain in one home so that her "tonic seizure activity" can be evaluated.

August 31, 2005 – Raye Dawn takes Kelsey to Dr. Koons for her Hepatitis A shot. Raye Dawn calls DHS to report Kelsey's progress and the fact that she's eating well.

September 1, 2005 – Raye Dawn takes Kelsey to Dr. Koons. CHBS visits Kelsey, Raye Dawn, and family at their home.

September 2, 2005 – An application for an emergency order is filed by the District Attorney requesting that unsupervised visits with Ashley be discontinued so Kelsey's seizure activity can be monitored. A hearing is set for September 8, 2005 to determine if visitation will be stopped. The application has a letter from the child's doctor attached. CHBS visits Kelsey, Raye Dawn, and family at their home.

September 2, 2005 – Ashley calls DHS concerning her visitation being suspended. The DHS worker informs her that there would be a hearing on September 8, 2005 to determine visitation.

September 4, 2005 – The Porter family goes to Frontier City in Oklahoma City where Kelsey rides many different rides. The question has been raised of the possibility that the impact of the rides could have caused the blunt force trauma to the abdomen and re-injured the internal injuries from the auto accident.

September 6, 2005 – Kelsey has a self-inflicted eye injury after rubbing adult shampoo out of her eye. CHBS and DHS visit Kelsey, Raye Dawn, and family at their home at two separate times during the day.

September 7, 2005 – CASA visits Kelsey, Raye Dawn, and family at their home.

September 8, 2005 – I hear the case to terminate visitation rights. Nobody from the paternal family shows at the hearing. Not even their attorney. The DA's office and Kelsey's attorney make a motion to dismiss Kelsey's case because things are going so well. This would have been three months after I had given her back. The motion is withdrawn after I take them in chambers and they read the Ryan Luke's law that says a deprived child case cannot be dismissed until six months after a child is returned to his or her parents. I rule as follows:

- No unsupervised visits with any of the Briggs family members, except for with Lance
- CASA to be able to talk to CHBS

September 13, 2005 – CHBS goes with Raye Dawn to Children's Hospital in Oklahoma City for a doctor's appointment.

> September 8, 2005 — I hear the case to terminate visitation rights. Nobody from the paternal family shows at the hearing.

September 20, 2005 – Raye Dawn takes Kelsey to Dr. Koons.

September 22, 2005 – CHBS visits Kelsey, Raye Dawn, and family at their home.

September 23, 2005 – Lance calls DHS with questions about Kelsey. He had been injured while driving a truck in Iraq and was in the United States. He wants Kelsey delivered to the airport to see him when he returns to Oklahoma.

September 27, 2005 – CHBS goes with Raye Dawn to Children's Hospital in Oklahoma City for a doctor's appointment.

September 30, 2005 – DHS visits Kelsey, Raye Dawn, and family at their home.

October 4, 2005 – CHBS visits Kelsey, Raye Dawn, and family at their home.

October 6, 2005 – CHBS visits Kelsey, Raye Dawn, and family at their home. Raye Dawn reports to DHS that Kelsey was heard saying "Never see mommy again. Never see grandma again." When asked where she heard those words, Kelsey responded "That girl."

October 6, 2005 – Lance calls DHS and informs them that he lied about his whereabouts and that he had been in Fort Benning, Georgia since September 21, 2005 and not in Iraq.

October 7, 2005 – Yolanda, a DHS worker, visits Kelsey's home and finds she is improving. Kelsey runs and hugs Yolanda.

October 11, 2005 – CHBS, makes a house visit and finds Kelsey to be fine. There is a turtle by her car and Kelsey and Raye Dawn take the turtle to the porch where Kelsey plays with it.

Later that day, October 11, 2005 – Kelsey is rushed to hospital with blunt force trauma to her stomach. She died.

Reform

It seems every state suffers from tragedies within their child welfare systems. The State of Oklahoma is no different. We need to focus on meaningful reform, if we are going to attack this problem. I have included these suggestions, and hope that from discussion more changes will follow.

- One of the biggest problems in the Kelsey Smith-Briggs case was the competing doctors' diagnosis regarding her broken legs. In cases such as these, a team of physicians with special training in child abuse and neglect would be available to provide expert consultation at the request of the Court or the Child's Attorney.

- Kelsey's law provides for DHS, the DA, the child's attorney, or the judge to call the Oklahoma State Bureau of Investigation to investigate injuries of a child. The difficulty with this type of investigation is it requires specialized training and results in additional costs. The legislature would need to properly fund this team, so the OSBI is not required to choose between a child abuse team and their regular agents. This is the only way additional investigations can be required, beyond DHS or the DA calling local enforcement.

- We need to allow the Oklahoma Commission on Children and Youth (OCCY) a more active role in deprived cases. The OCCY acts as the watch dog for DHS, but maybe more than a watchdog is needed. Allow them to be another set of eyes on the child. However, once again, if we are going to create the work, we must budget the pay. In other words, the legislature must fully fund OCCY.

- We need to create specified neglect teams within DHS in an effort to remove filth from the child, not the child from the filth. We do not have enough special teams such as CHBS to go into homes and train parents on how to break the cycle of neglect. In the last several years repeat contacts with neglected children has caused more deaths than physical abuse.

- Finally, if we are going to be serious about reforming the system, let's stop making the high profile cases or reform targets. In 2005 there were 52 deaths, but only one was reported. Why? What changes were necessary in the other 51 cases to give us the best chance to avoid those deaths?

It is a sad reality that all of the reform and all of the programs will not stop these kinds of tragedies. Ultimately, we must reform families to obtain the desired results.

Glossary

Actual Physical Control (APC) of a motor vehicle while intoxicated -An APC is when a person is in an operable vehicle with a blood alcohol concentration above the legal limit

Assistant District Attorney (ADA) – An attorney employed by the District Attorney's office to prosecute crimes

Associate District Judge – A judge whose jurisdiction is limited to the county where elected

Case Worker – A Department of Human Services worker who carries a caseload of abused and neglected children

Comprehensive Home Based Services (CHBS) – A service that visits at risk children in their homes in order to help protect them

Court Appointed Special Advocates (CASA) – Volunteers who advocate for children and are appointed by the court to the family

Custody – A parent or guardian who has the legal obligation and responsibility to care for a child

Department of Human Services (DHS) – Oklahoma State's division of child protective and family welfare services

Deprived Child Petition – The legal document that alleges a child is either abused, neglected, or both, and should be made a ward of the court

District Attorney (DA) – Chief Law enforcement officer of the district, and as such is the prosecutor for the district

Guardian ad litem – An attorney appointed to represent a child's best interest in a legal proceeding

Guardianship – Court appointed individual to care for the person and property of a minor or incapacitated person who cannot care for themselves

Hearing – A court proceeding

Individualized Treatment Plan – Provides a parent the conditions required to correct in order to have their child returned to them

OCCY – Oklahoma Commission on Children and Youth

Glossary

Project Safe – A non-profit corporation that provides services to the citizens of Lincoln and Pottawatomie Counties in Oklahoma for victims of domestic violence

Protective Order – An order issued by a judge requiring a person not to come around, harm, or harass another individual

Victim's Compensation Account (VCA) – Money paid by criminal defendants to an account that provides fine compensations to victims of crimes